Start At Square One

Starting and Managing the Planned Gift Program

Lynda S. Moerschbaecher

Precept Press, Chicago
A Division of Bonus Books, Inc.

02   01   00   99   98   5   4   3   2   1

Library of Congress Cataloging-in-Publication Data

Moerschbaecher, Lynda S.
Start at square one: starting and managing the planned gift
program / Lynda S. Moerschbaecher.
p   .cm.
Includes bibliographical references and index.
ISBN 1-56625-089-7
1. Deferred giving—United States. 2. Fund raising—United
States. 3. Nonprofit organizations—United States. I. Title.
HV41.9.U5M64 1997
658,15′224—dc21

97-26588

Precept Press
Divison of Bonus Books, Inc.
160 East Illinois Street
Chicago, Illinois 60611

Printed in the United States of America

Table of Contents

From The Author

In confronting the task of putting together her life experiences in some semblance of order and meaning in *West with the Night*, Beryl Markham was uncertain how to begin bringing together all the things she wanted to say. She pondered:

> How is it possible to bring order out of memory? I should like to begin at the beginning, patiently, like a weaver at his loom. I should like to say, 'This is the place to start: there can be no other.'

I face a similar task in bringing together thoughts from my consulting and law practices in which I have worked exclusively with planned gifts and planned giving programs for over twenty years. Where do I start? I can now appreciate the thoughts of another author known to many of you, Jerold Panas, who said at the outset of his book *Born to Raise*: "When I started this book, I had all the answers. By the time I had completed it, I wasn't even sure of the questions." I agree.

Foreword

I n my practice of law I have had the opportunity to meet many extremely successful business people and nonprofit leaders, from corporate managers to board volunteers. I have observed that in undertaking a new endeavor, these people tend to exhibit a common pattern of thinking, a common approach to success.

It falls into three phases: (1) they think the endeavor through, exercising creative visualization of the program by learning what they need to know and philosophizing about it; (2) they plan carefully both in thought and in writing — thorough analyses, business plans and marketing plans; (3) they immediately implement their well-laid plans.

Because we can all learn a great deal from the success of others, I have employed the same approach to sort out the process of creating a dynamic planned gift program. The chapters ahead are divided into three general sections: Think, Plan and Implement.

I wish you great success in following this tried and true method of achieving your goals, whether they are personal or fund-raising goals.

Introduction

Creating or even revitalizing a planned giving program is akin to starting a new business. It needs to move through many stages of "process" before it becomes profitable.

Many steps in the process involve underlying work designed to build a firm foundation, which permits the "product" to be successfully presented to the public without encountering major snags, flaws or legal liability. There can be moments when it all seems not quite worth the effort; frustration and budgetary woes are bound to be part of the process for *every* institution. But, just as with a new business, the moment arrives when it all starts to come together and you see the results, when you realize the work and persistence has truly paid off.

Too often, however, the process is skipped over and an organization suddenly announces that it has a planned giving program. On what basis does it make this claim?

Let's look at examples of the low-budget and the high-budget operation. In each case, the examples are true stories.

Low-budget. A development director told me he was simply too busy at the moment to consider planned giving, but he said it was definitely on his agenda this year. I asked what he planned to do within this twelve-month period. "Oh, when we're ready for it," he replied, "we'll do a donor seminar."

Assuming he would fortuitously invite the right prospects, select the right topics and invite the right speakers, I wondered what he would do if a prospect came to him after the seminar and said, "You know, that seems to fit my situation. I'd like to contribute to your pooled income fund."

What if he had to respond that his organization doesn't yet have a pooled income fund? Would he simply say that after it was drafted by an attorney and approved by the board, and after the investment objective, set by the finance committee, and the SEC disclosure statement were written and adopted, they could accept the gift?

Or, what if the prospect were to say, "I'm thinking of setting up such a trust, but only have $100,000. The trustee fees are too steep at the bank. Will you act as trustee?"

Or, "I have a piece of real estate with a small mortgage. I own it with a partner. Can you take that as payment on my pledge to the campaign?"

After I posed these potential situations, the development director admitted he had never thought of those things. What if you don't have your pooled income fund in place or haven't discussed, accepting the legal liability of trusteeship? What if you haven't set up a procedure for reviewing, accepting and marketing the real estate, not to mention a partnership interest, a mortgage and hazardous waste (quite separate from the question of gift crediting)?

The point is, face-to-face contact with donors and prospects is about one-tenth of your job as a planned giving officer. The underlying preparatory work — program design, prospect identification, drafting of a business plan, marketing, use of professionals to leverage your contacts, relations with other departments of the institution, pricing gift opportunities through planned gifts and many more things — will make or break your job.

Consider again a start-up business. Let's imagine one, say a shoe store. Could a new shoe store just order a load of shoes and begin selling them? Certainly not. Is there even an actual store to sell from? Are there systems for buying, selling, recording, checking inventory, paying wages, covering overhead, handling taxes, etc.? Much thought and planning must be undertaken before you can ever offer shoes for sale if you intend to have a successful, long-term operation. And so it is with a successful planned giving office.

High-budget. I went to lunch with a planned giving officer hired by a hospital to start a planned giving program. She told me she bought the Teitell deferred giving reference books and the R&R Newkirk reference set. She also said she would soon be getting a newsletter and purchasing brochures and mailers.

She said the hospital currently offered absolutely every-thing — CRATs, CRUTs, CGAs, DGAs, CLTs, PIFs, retained life estates and installment bargain sales. She said prior to this job she read both *Charitable Gift Planning News* and *Taxwise Giving* every month and was ready for anything. She was truly motivat-ed. I asked how she had done so far in bringing in gifts — the ul-timate truth. She said she was actually dismayed that she hadn't yet closed a single gift. I told her she was "over-vehicled;" that she needed a program, a strategy. She needed the "process" of getting gifts.

Outside seller of gifts. In recent years, many organizations seeking the "quick fix" have engaged an outside "seller" to bring in planned gifts, particularly CRTs. The organization is usually approached by a person who promises or contracts to close numerous gifts valued well into the millions.

The organization is generally asked to part with current dollars it already owns and could use right now, so that it can acquire a larger amount in *deferred* dollars. Often, on a present value basis, the future value of the funds coming to the charity is hardly greater, if at all, than the funds it gives up in exchange. In addition, once the "seller" of gifts departs from the scene, the or-ganization is left empty-handed, with no established planned giving program.

Who Becomes a Planned Giving Officer or Consultant?

A nonprofit organization is created to carry out a specific function related to the needs of our society or culture. Quite of-ten, the executive director has risen through the ranks of the substantive program as opposed to having been trained primari-ly as a manager, whether of a business, a governmental unit or a nonprofit organization. The development office, on the other hand, generally attracts people from the outside world, and of-ten those people possess or develop an entrepreneurial attitude.

The development office is a "profit center" within a *non-*

profit organization. Others in the institution do not always understand this mentality. At the same time, development officers who transfer to a nonprofit from the outside sometimes have little patience for or understanding of a bureaucratic nonprofit process that prevents them from moving quickly to motivate donors or accept certain gifts (e.g. real estate).

The development office imposes a "bottom-line" mentality on an organization not geared to profits. Values dear to most nonprofits — equity, fairness, meeting the needs of all — are often obstacles to entrepreneurial ventures. Therefore, fund raisers, and particularly planned giving personnel, must exist in two worlds simultaneously: the money/business world of donors, and the "non-money" world of the substantive efforts of nonprofit organizations. The tensions that arise from this conflict in cultures cause more daily problems than we may realize at first.

Planned giving staff deal with high dollar amounts and wealthy donors while living in the little office at the end of the hall with indoor-outdoor carpeting and metal furniture (or worse, they live off-site). Colleagues in the nonprofit may have trouble understanding the dichotomy or stress this situation may produce. Often, faculty of a school, hospital personnel, staff of the environmental organization or social workers have little sympathy for the problems of the wealthy and may, in fact, disdain that wealth.

Meanwhile, the major gifts or planned gifts officer must maintain a balance between this attitude and the reality of dealing with a donor of wealth. Too often, the nonprofit staff feels it is the social responsibility of the wealthy to fund the organization in question. This attitude can make cooperation difficult to come by when the planned gifts officer wants special consideration from management or other staff persons in the gift structuring or gift acceptance process for a donor of wealth.

In light of the potential for such conflict and tension, who is inclined to accept a position as a planned giving officer? Consider the following possibilities:

(1)   The so-called "migrant worker," the sales-oriented de-

velopment type with no loyalty to the particular organization, perhaps the former salesperson of a product or an intangible.

(2) The person with an emotional need to "do good."

(3) The person who loves a particular institution (loyalty to it may be part of a family tradition, or the organization may be "family" to the person).

(4) The person who transfers into planned giving because s/he is "burned-out" by another profession or another part of the institution.

(5) The person who is assigned to planned giving without being given much of a choice.

(6) Considering the profession's recent growth, the person interested in planned giving as a job or profession (someone perhaps fascinated by its technical concepts).

From the point of view of the person entering planned giving, this may sound discouraging. On the other hand, realism about the job, and its requirements, will help the person adjust and perhaps lead to more job satisfaction and less job turnover. Not all of the job is interfacing with wealthy prospects and structuring million dollar gifts with fancy techniques. Much of it involves basic fund-raising principles that other areas of fund raising have mastered so well. Perhaps a better understanding of these would help prevent the reported twenty-four month turnover in planned giving jobs.

In addition, understanding what may lie ahead allows time for planning, to both avoid conflicts and help create an atmosphere conducive to a successful planned giving program.

From the organization's point of view, the choice of a planned giving officer is, needless to say, an essential element in the success of the program. Organizations often ask which candidate is preferable, a marketing-oriented person or a technically-oriented person. It is my opinion that the question is irrelevant, and that other qualities should be sought.

Generally, the person should understand philanthropy, the role it has played historically in building this country, the role it currently plays and its future trends. Specifically, s/he must thoroughly understand the program the organization delivers and be committed to it. Commitment is always asked of board members, while staff persons, who are the backbone of the operation, are often treated as "hired guns." This may be one factor in the high turnover rate of development office employees.

Personal abilities to look for in a planned giving officer might include the following: someone who (1) is good-humored, pleasant and determined; (2) does not let constant disruption, negativity, rejection and shoestring budgets bother him/her; (3) while making $65,000 per year, will try to understand what it means for others to part with a half-million dollars; (4) will try to understand the psychology of the wealthy without ever exhibiting jealousy or insensitivity to their special needs, and will never call a donor "Mrs. Gotrocks;" (5) is willing to learn extensive amounts of confusing information which will change just as soon as it is learned; and (6) has a "presence" that will be accepted by donors of wealth and professional advisors.

The philosophy of this book is to help you discover the "process," and to help you successfully get that process underway so that it leads you toward developing an effective, long-term planned giving program. If you *Start at Square One,* the gifts will follow your well-laid plans.

SECTION ONE

"THINK"

What is the Planned Giving Program and Where Does It Fit?

Someone remarked on the huge number of failures Edison had encountered in his search for a new storage battery — fifty thousand experiments before he achieved results. 'Results?' said the inventor. 'Why, I have gotten a lot of results. I know fifty thousand things that won't work.'

I f you are thinking about or planning to set up a planned giving program, STOP RIGHT NOW. Please do not select a planned giving committee! That could be the death knell of your new program, or at least the ball and chain around your ankle for a long time to come.

I would like to tell you exactly how to start your planned giving program and exactly how long it will take for it to be successful. By the end of this book, I hope to do just that. But before we get into the thick of it, you must realize there are many interwoven issues we need to address first.

Sure, many consultants encourage a cookie-cutter approach to planned giving, but beware of the temptation of easy implementation. Because organizations are as different as snowflakes, creating an effective program involves more than an exercise in enthusiasm coupled with purchased or purloined materials.

People in advertising tell us there are certain words that always lure us into a product or service — easy, proven, guaranteed, success, free, fast, etc. In fact, you could probably write an ad with just these words — "Here is the easy, proven way to guaranteed success in planned giving. It's fast and nearly free!"

Many theories exist as to the best (and easiest) way to create a truly successful planned giving program. None is completely' right or completely wrong. You need to listen to several peoples' ideas. But don't waste too much time theorizing, action will be more effective for bringing in planned gifts.

But "how," you might ask, when you do not have a clue where and how to start. To paraphrase Beryl Markham, this is the place to start, there can be no other. It starts with you.

I would like to pass along the wisdom of a couple of other people and/or organizations who know nothing about planned giving, but everything about how to start a planned giving program.

First, like the Nike ads say, just do it. There is no substitute for jumping in feet first. Please do not say to yourself, "But I'm a one-person development office. Where will I find the time to do all you say I must do?" The clients that I have convinced to "just do it" now have millions, eight-figure millions, in their planned giving portfolio. And, their annual gifts have increased dramatically, as has the planned giving program's portion of the capital campaign.

The next comment I often hear is, "But they are in large organizations and their fund raising is more developed." Not true. Some of those clients are in fact very small schools, hospitals, church-related organizations and many other types of nonprofits whose fund-raising program *became* better developed, easier and more organized as a result of their planned giving effort.

You can go on with excuses if you wish, and say, "But I don't know anything about planned giving." That is not true either. If you know anything about fund raising and fund-raising principles, you already know a great deal about planned giving. If you come from a marketing or sales background, you already know a great deal about a different side of planned giving. If you come from the tax technical or financial world, you know yet another facet of planned giving.

Fund raising, marketing and technical aspects comprise the three-legged stool on which planned giving sits. *You have a starting point and so does your organization.* I intend to show you just where your starting point is — which leads me to the next person of wisdom, Steven Covey.

Mr. Covey, in *The Seven Habits of Highly Successful People*, says to begin with the end in mind. To begin with the end in mind means to start with a clear understanding of your destination. To know where you're going gives you a better understanding of where you are now. It also helps you determine the steps you need to take, and forces you in the right direction with spirit and confidence.

The end goal of this plan is to develop a new, large and growing source of revenue for the organization by means of a program that is affordable.

If this is your end goal, it is of ultimate importance to you to understand what revenue the organization has now, and from what sources it is derived. You also need to know what it costs for the organization to attain it. Then you need to offer the organization *much* more of it — yes, not a little but a lot — through your program and at a respectably low cost.

To do this, you must start by understanding the sources of revenue for a nonprofit and the sources of revenue for your organization. Every nonprofit has the potential to gain revenue from five generic sources and can expend it in three end uses of the funds. You need to understand sources and uses of funds; you also need to know exactly where your particular organization's money comes from (sources of gross revenues), and you need to know its net revenue after expenses and where it goes (end uses). This information will help you form a clear picture of how to prepare your own program. This information will both place your revenue-raising effort in perspective and, especially, will convince your Board and CEO to advance substantial amounts of money to your new project.

One of the most difficult tasks in starting a planned giving program is getting upper management to listen to your needs and then to act on them. But there is a way to accomplish this. It is called a positive bottom line — showing management an unbelievable yield on a dollar invested in your program as compared to a dollar invested in any other program of the organization, whether for carrying out the charitable purpose or for any other type of fund-raising effort. Significant dollars speak significantly to your board and management.

The next wise person you need to listen to is Yogi Berra, who said if you don't know where you are going, it may be difficult to get there. No fooling. A planned giving program without goals, revenue projections, projected yield on money invested in the program, activity schedules, a business plan and a marketing plan, will not convince anyone that you really can achieve phenomenal success. Neither can you simply take gifts "over the transom."

Gift receiving and a program to continually promote an ongoing flow of gifts are two different things. Eventually, you want this to be a *program* or, as Webster's Dictionary says, "the plan or procedure for dealing with some matter." In other words, you need to get an infrastructure established to carry on your work for you.

Somers White of Phoenix, Arizona, a speaking and business consultant I have used, once asked me to tell him truthfully if I feel I have experienced success in what I do. After the usual hemming and hawing, telling him I needed to define success, etc., he stopped me and said to just tell him in one word, yes or no. I said yes. Then, he said, if that's the case you need to tell others how to do it as well. I told him it would take me the twenty years that I have been in business to do so. "I intend to get you to do it in just a few minutes," he replied. Cynic that I am, I said it was not possible.

He asked me to think for a moment and then tell him what *the most important factor* in achieving my success was. Just one thing, no more. I was puzzled. I could see he was not about to let me out of this little exercise, and I was clearly uncomfortable. I could not identify merely one thing that was the most important ingredient in my success. When I protested, he calmly told me to take as much time as I needed. So I sat at first stewing then realizing that we would go no further if I did not do this. So I thought long and hard and, after what seemed to be an inordinate amount of time, I finally broke the silence.

"I know what it is," I told him. "I saw what I could do, knew I could do it excellently and I set my heart to it. I told myself I had ten years to accomplish it."

"Great!" he said. At this point, I thought I had completed the exercise; instead he laid out another challenge. "Now, what is the second most important thing?" "Sir," I protested, "I'm not sure there is a second thing." He assured me there was. So again I thought and thought.

The second most important thing, I told him, was to begin planning the steps that would get me there, to determine the possible roads and avenues to this goal — understanding that part way down a road I might have to change direction at the next intersection, to adjust my course as I felt my way along.

"Great!" he said. "Now, what was the third most important thing?" I began to wonder how long this exercise would last and said, "I think you are being unfair. How many more things can I come up with?" But before he had a chance to respond, I told him the third most important thing was that I just got out there and did it.

He then summarized what I, unbeknownst to myself, had just said. "You set a goal you were committed to, you set up your plans to achieve it and then, most importantly, you implemented and took action to arrive there. Don't you see?" he said, "these are the three most important factors for anyone to achieve success. Now, it is your job to tell others."

Interestingly, he showed me I had done what Steven Covey says — begin with the end in mind. Then he showed me I had taken Yogi Berra's advice as well — get your road map together, or you won't know where you are going or how to get there. And finally, he convinced me I had done what Nike begs of us — just do it!

So, as a result of Mr. White's instruction, I learned. And now, I pass it along. In fact, for years now I have privately helped many organizations into very successful planned gift *programs* based on these principles.

In this book, I hope to put them in place for you, so you can take advantage of the same principles. Let's revisit the three sections of this book: *Think* (understand the end you wish to achieve), *Plan* (set up the road map for success) and *Implement* (what you need to do to "just do it"). This may not be the only way to achieve success in planned giving, but it is a proven way.

Starting With The End In Mind: The Planned Gifts You Will Have Brought In

Although our subject matter is the creation of a successful planned giving program, we cannot clearly focus on how to make such success a reality if we do not first address the fact that planned gift fund raising is merely one form of generating revenue for the nonprofit. This particular form of revenue generation must be understood in the context of all the sources of revenue and the nonprofit management's expenses. Money received obviously must exceed expenses, or at least be equal to expenses, if the nonprofit is to continue to exist.

It may never have occurred to you that to offer a fruitful planned giving program, you need to analyze the revenue generated by the whole organization. Such a study will focus your plans. It will also help management clearly see the time and resources that must be allocated to establish this very lucrative form of revenue generation. And, without question, you will be able to speak with confidence to prospects about the financial status of the organization.

Once you see the gross and net revenue from each of the five categories of overall revenue, you will need to analyze the sources specifically from the development office. Then, the true attributes of planned gift revenue generation must also be understood — some of the receipts will be current and others will be deferred until a later date. You will see that planned giving is best undertaken as a part of a consolidated effort within the development office, not as a mere adjunct program that does not functionally relate to the rest of development effort.

Since it will cost money up front to start this endeavor, the costs and benefits of the undertaking need to be understood and clearly laid out for management and the board of directors to see and evaluate. If those expenditures can be made to augment the coffers of other fund-raising endeavors, all the better.

Why Analyze Your Revenue from These Five Sources

Some people beginning in planned giving may question why it is necessary to analyze each and every source of revenue of the nonprofit when all they want to do is start a planned giving program. Senior people in the field who have been around for a while know that you will face all the objections management and boards can possibly raise against committing money and time to a new program. This book will help you convince management that there are certain essentials involved in starting this process — and that these essentials will lead to a healthy payoff.

You will need time, money, commitment, cooperation and resources to get your program up and running. You cannot do it alone, that I guarantee. You need the support of the rest of the development office, the business office, the CEO's office and the board. Before outlining the "how to get it," let me explain how I came to understand all of this myself.

Over a decade ago, I was working with a local hospital to help the development office show the Foundation Board that it could, indeed, handle a planned giving effort. At that time, the typical method was to set up a planned giving committee and start having meetings. Of course, the first thing a committee needs is a chair, right? So, the committee elected one. It happened to be the CEO of a local bank. Next, the development officer (one-person shop) and I made a presentation to the committee as to what planned giving is, what the gift vehicles are and so on. But nothing happened. The committee was not sure this was the right thing for *this* hospital at *this* time, a story I had heard many times before.

We persisted, however, in having meetings until the committee chair, the banker, finally said that we had not convinced him.

He needed to know what the yield would be on the funds advanced by the board for this new effort, and how much, in terms of actual dollars, would be received over the next five years. As to the budget we had prepared, he pointed out that we had only prepared the expense side, but not the revenue side. As a businessman, he refused to make a fool of himself by taking this to the Foundation Board, of which he was the chair, let alone the Hospital Board, for approval of the funds when the Hospital Board, on which he sat, knew all too well the other priority calls on its money. New facilities, expensive equipment, education of employees, employee benefits, fighting competition, etc., were all needed right away. To spend funds on a program that would possibly pay off in the future, but had no guarantees, was just not what he could honestly present to the board as a worthwhile place to invest the next dollar.

We responded with the typical planned giving community response, that it would take three to five years to realize a revenue stream from this effort and that it would be impossible to set dollar goals. We were happy to set activity goals, however. But he would not budge.

He offered to take this to the Hospital Board **if** we could show him a business plan that he, as a banker, would be willing to lend on. That was his ultimatum; make this as solid a proposal as we would if we went to his bank for a loan — we were asking for $500,000 over five years. We proceeded to work on it and called a few more meetings before he put a halt to the meetings, saying we were just not coming up with what he needed to propose to the board (a proposal as if this were the board of his bank).

After the meeting, I pulled him aside and said I was at my wit's end as a consultant, that I had done all I knew how to do in good faith. I asked him how I could get a $500,000 loan from his bank for a new business, when that business did not yet exist. How in the world could I prove to him what he wanted? I requested a meeting with him at his bank. He agreed to it.

The meeting at the bank went extremely well. In fact, at the next committee meeting we called, the development officer and I presented a business plan just as the banker had taught me. Within ten minutes of presenting it, a committee member, the CFO of the hospital, said, "Look at this, I'll bet we could do $4,000,000 in planned gifts within three years." The banker had not said a word. The rest of the committee agreed with the CFO and they all said they really wanted to try this. One member turned to the banker and said, "You have really been an opponent of spending the hospital's money on this program, but I think the rest of us have come to the conclusion that this program is worth it. I think we are willing to take that leap of faith based on this information, are you?" The banker said yes, and they were off and running.

Can you develop such compelling information? The answer is "yes."

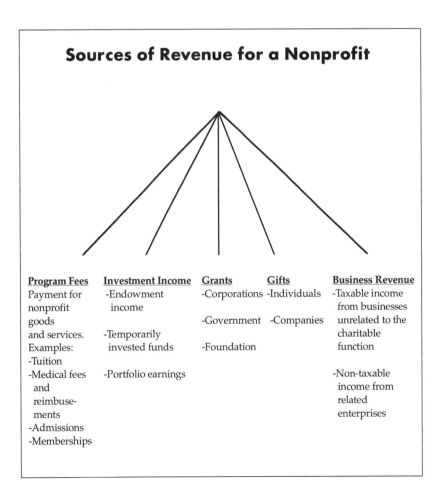

Sources of Revenue for a Nonprofit

Program Fees	Investment Income	Grants	Gifts	Business Revenue
Payment for nonprofit goods and services. Examples:	-Endowment income	-Corporations	-Individuals	-Taxable income from businesses unrelated to the charitable function
-Tuition	-Temporarily invested funds	-Government	-Companies	
-Medical fees and reimbusements	-Portfolio earnings	-Foundation		-Non-taxable income from related enterprises
-Admissions				
-Memberships				

How to Analyze Your Revenue
from These Five Sources

You may be in for some interesting surprises when you use this chart to analyze your organization's funds. You may even begin to note some important trends and shifts from year to year. Generally, financial records are not kept on this basis, so a little work needs to be done to categorize the revenues in this manner. The result, however, will be a better understanding of your starting point for any new program in any one of these five categories.

Look at the five generic sources of revenue that any nonprofit may have. The first one is the gross revenue derived from carrying out the program, for which it is tax-exempt. For example, a school has tuition, a hospital has patient revenue and third party reimbursements, a museum has admissions.

The second is income earned on investments, which may include interest income, dividends, rental income, royalties and other unearned or passive income. Funds may be held for temporary investment, whether days, months or even years. Or funds may be invested permanently, which may be endowment, of one sort or another. Some such funds are restricted and others are unrestricted in the accounting sense. The types of endowment will be addressed later in this chapter.

The third is revenue from grants which, although generally from the development effort, are completely different in nature from gifts. One thing you will become accustomed to by the end of this book is that in the donor-donee context, there is a consumer and a producer of gift opportunities. Your organization offers gift opportunities, therefore it is a producer. A donor takes that opportunity for him/herself, and is therefore a consumer of the gift opportunity. In the world of grants, from corporations, foundations and government, the consumer of the gift opportunity is a very sophisticated buyer. The grant-maker does this every day. In a sense they are professional donors. That is reflected in the fact that the "gift," given in the form of a grant, is more like a contract. It has parameters to follow and expectations as to usage, reporting and the like. For this reason, grants are a different type of revenue than true gifts. The tax law calls true gifts acts of "detached and disinterested generosity."

Gifts that are truly gratuitous (even though they may be designed and earmarked to support a particular purpose) are generally from individuals, although corporations and some foundations may give "detached and disinterested" gifts, too. These individual gifts comprise the fourth category. These donors are not professional consumers of your gift opportunities. Thus, in this category, at least for this analysis, I suggest you include only individuals' gifts. Include in this revenue source all types of individual gifts, as we will further break out later — annual, major (including planned and deferred), special events and special appeals.

The fifth, and last, generic source of revenue is related and unrelated enterprises. This source, as opposed to investment income, is active income from the operation of a trade or business. Some businesses are related to the function for which the organization has its exemption from income taxes and are, therefore, also exempt from taxation, or they may be unrelated to the purpose for which the nonprofit has its exemption and are, therefore, taxable as unrelated business income.

You will need to work with your CFO to develop the numbers for each of these categories. They are generally not kept in this manner, but are accessible from the books and records of the institution. I have found the CFOs to be very interested in the results of this study for their own purposes.

Once you have a gross revenue figure for each of the categories, put it at the top of the category on the chart, above the five sources. Next, at the bottom of the chart — on the "bottom line," so to speak — fill in the net revenue amount from each category. Net revenue will be the gross revenue less the directly related expenses to produce that revenue. You will find some CFOs will choose to add in proportionate indirect costs to each category. Question them on the basis of the allocation to each source of revenue for fairness of amounts attributable to development.

Then stand back and take a look. Program revenue rarely completely supports the activity of the nonprofit. If it does, the profit margin is generally fairly slim and is sometimes nonexistent. Calculate the **yield** on this category by dividing the net revenue by the gross revenue. For example, if the gross revenue for the program income is $20,000,000 and the net figure is $1,200,000, the yield on the next dollar invested in this type of activity is six percent ($1,200,000 divided by $20,000,000). Investing the organization's funds to generate another dollar in this category will yield a six percent return.

Do the same for each of the five categories. You will probably find that the investment category has anywhere from a six percent yield to a twenty-five percent total rate of return, if yield plus capital growth is counted in the investment result. Related businesses may have a higher yield than unrelated businesses (if the organization has any of this type of activity at all). That is because the unrelated business income is taxed at the rate of corporations, if the nonprofit is a corporation, or at the rate of a trust, if the nonprofit is organized as a trust. In either event, the tax rate will cause a significant decrease in the yield on the dollar invested in this type of activity. Related business yield may run thirty to forty percent, while taxable business yields are probably more in the range of ten to twenty percent.

Now look at the results of the gifts and grants. First they are together if the same department runs them, and then they are separated out into their own categories. Whereas the resulting yields in each of the other three categories range from negative to perhaps thirty percent or so, the yield on the dollar spent in this area is more in the range of 900 percent for a shop that has a budget of $200,000 with fund-raising revenue of $2,000,000, to a range of 940 percent for a shop running on a budget of $300,000 raising $5,000,000. This latter example may include closed and vested planned gifts that have not yet matured, but to which the institution is entitled.

This raises a question of whether to count these gifts for this analysis at their current present value of the remainder interest, or to count them at face value, if they are of the deferred type. For this purpose, do not count revocable gifts. Even if deferred gifts are counted at present value, you will probably find a range of 500 percent, and well above, for the yield on the dollar invested in this activity. For example, assume the development office spending

$200,000 and bringing in $2,000,000 raised $1,000,000 of that in deferred gifts, and assume the typical remainder value is thirty-five to forty percent. The value earned was, let us say, $1,400,000 ($1,000,000 in outright gifts plus $400,000 of present value of deferred gifts). With expenses at $200,000, this is still a yield of 857 percent. In the second development office mentioned above, if the $5,000,000 was $2,500,000 in current gifts and $2,500,000 in deferred gifts with the same approximate remainder value of forty percent, the revenue total would be $3,500,000 ($2,500,000 plus $1,000,000) on a present value basis, with expenses of $300,000. The yield is still 914 percent.

Even if you are taking deferred gifts from younger donors and the average remainder value is only twenty percent, in the example of the $2,000,000 development office, where $1,000,000 is from deferred gifts (counted at their $200,000 present value), the total revenue is $1,200,000 and the expenses are $200,000. This yield is still 833 percent. How can you beat that?

This depiction of the organization's revenue alone should show management that it would be well-considered to invest the next dollar in this area of revenue production. Would they prefer a yield of six percent or 1000 percent on their next dollar invested in the organization? I have joked to more than one board of directors that the fund-raising effort from individuals pays such a high net on the gross revenue that they should consider abandoning the nonprofit program and just have a fund-raising office.

Do this analysis. Don't hesitate and do it with your CFO. Write up a report for you, the VP of Development and the CEO. The CFO will already know the numbers, but copy him or her on the report. This is the first step in the discipline that is absolutely necessary for developing a wonderful, lucrative planned gift effort.

We should not stop here, however. We should further break down the development office revenue. This is a healthy exercise, if only for the Vice President of Development or the Director of Development, whoever manages the five fields of revenue in the development office. For the CEO and the board, it is important to show the yield on major gifts as opposed to annual or special events. This yield on major gifts is the highest yield and serves to convince them that, within the development effort, the best use of the next dollar is in the major gift area.

Development Office Revenue

Gift revenue derives from programs, within the development office, designed to acquire revenue from existing or newly acquired donors. Development programs are efforts directed in different manners to achieving the same goal: obtaining gratuitous funding to keep the organization operational. It is important to keep in mind that each of the various types of revenue programs have a common goal, namely a better and bigger bottom line for the organization. Lack of understanding of this common goal is the source of many woes in the development office.

Development Revenue

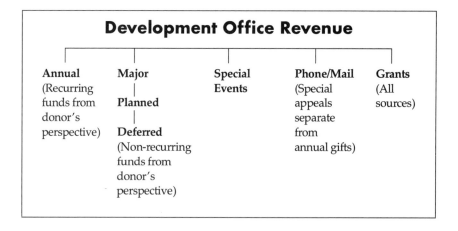

Development Office Revenue

Annual	Major	Special	Phone/Mail	Grants
(Recurring funds from donor's perspective)	**Planned**	Events	(Special appeals separate from annual gifts)	(All sources)
	Deferred (Non-recurring funds from donor's perspective)			

Every well-rounded development office has established programs in these five areas, even though all such programs may be staffed by only one or two people and these efforts may be called by completely different names than those shown on the chart. In considering the interrelationship of the programs' recurring and nonrecurring sources of revenue, the pieces of the development office must be viewed from a different perspective than the usual fare if a planned giving program is to be put into place. Planned giving cannot be an adjunct; it must be an integral part of the overall fund-raising process. You must be willing to change your view on certain long-held "beliefs" about the development office.

Our impressions and perceptions and the view taken or espoused over long periods of time lead us to believe that there are such things as annual gifts, major gifts and planned gifts. But we know that all gifts are planned; no gift is by accident. So let us start with what really differentiates the annual gift from the major or planned gift. We might call one a "recurring gift" while calling the other a "nonrecurring gift." Although we know that a major or planned gift may, in fact, recur, it does not often do so. And, when this type of gift does recur, it does not necessarily go to the same donee. You will note the term I use here is *nonrecurring*, rather than never-recurring.

We need to look at the gift process from the point of view of the donor and not be so myopic as to constantly see things from our own, perhaps arrogant, point of view. Surely, the terms "annual," "major" and "deferred" are simply for our own administrative convenience. They mean nothing at all to a donor. On the other hand, a gift that "recurs" frequently versus one that is nonrecurring or seldom recurring may be better understood by the donor, the person who foots the bill. Also, in the same vein, if a donor realizes that s/he is making a "nonrecurring" gift, s/he also understands the significance and magnitude of the gift. So why can't we change our focus to the donor's point of view? The donor will understand that there are recurring and nonrecurring *funding* needs. This also aids in keeping the two separate for the purpose of continuing the flow of recurring gifts for recurring needs, even while the donor makes a nonrecurring gift for a nonrecurring purpose.

The shift of our focus to the donor's point of view will result in a number of positive changes. First, the parts of the development office will be easier to coordinate because they understand the larger picture on the donor's side and when s/he may be ready or not ready to make a large gift. Information can be shared more easily. The donor does not get asked for conflicting support. And, perhaps best of all, the donor understands that when s/he is asked to commit to the "nonrecurring" gift, s/he is being asked something very special — to become the equivalent of a *shareholder* of the organization. But that does not mean recurring needs have gone away.

In addition to the coordination of the parts for the convenience of the approach to the donor, an understanding of the five parts of development revenue production will also give rise to an understanding of how to use information gathered in other programs (within the five parts of the development office) to create internal markets for any other of the five parts. This is especially helpful for the new planned giving program.

Now, take the five parts of the development revenue source and do the same that you have with the overall revenue of the organization. That is, calculate the gross revenue from each type of revenue generator, allocate the direct expenses (and possibly the indirect overhead) of raising that revenue to the category and determine your bottom line for each one. Next, determine your yield, as we did above, for the organization's overall revenue. This should give you a good look at the health of each part and where you should be placing valuable staff time and precious resources. If you only read this and think about it, and never get around to doing it because you "know enough" about it anyway, I predict you will not have great success in planned giving. Put a pencil to paper or mouse or keyboard to computer and "just do it." You may actually enjoy the understanding that it gives you of your development effort.

Major Gift Revenue

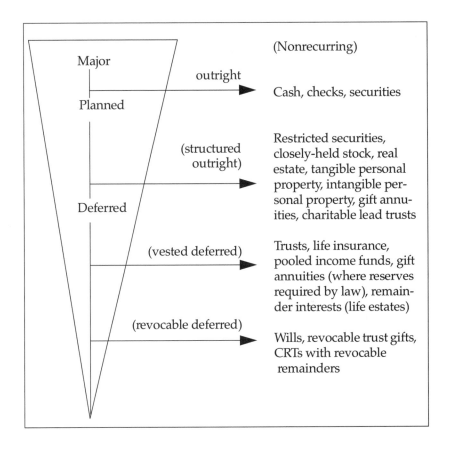

Let us look more closely at the gift we typically call a major gift. Most organizations arbitrarily set a dollar figure as its major gift level, for example $5,000. However, if we take the donor's perspective, that is simply not true for all donors. You may have one donor who regularly gives (a recurring gift) $100 for whom a $5,000 gift is truly a stretch and indeed a major gift. Compare this to the donor who *regularly* gives you $5,000. Is this really a major gift for that person? Clearly not. For him/her it would take a much larger gift, something in the nature of $100,000 or more, to be a *nonrecurring* gift. Obviously, the fund-raising industry categorizes major gift levels in dollar amounts for their own administrative convenience, not because it has anything at all to do with the donor's capacity or intent to give or to support one kind of need versus another.

However, to make sense of where planned giving fits with both existing annual gift programs and existing major gift programs, you will need to reconsider how we look at these terms. Planned giving will make sense, plain and clear, if you go along with these terms and meanings, at least for the moment. You may not wish to change your administrative structures, but you will need to stretch your mind to embrace these new concepts. If you do, many of the startup woes other organizations experience will vanish.

If a major gift is a nonrecurring gift of larger proportions than one could give regularly, then all parts of the above chart, including planned and deferred giving, are part of major giving (whether or not the organizational structure of the development office reflects this). This manner of viewing major gifts will also permit you a clear understanding of the difference between *planned* and *deferred* gifts.

First, how does the major gift differ from the planned gift? You can see that the major gift is cash, checks, marketable securities or liquid assets. The planned gift requires structure and design to achieve the best benefits and to conform to the requirements of the law. It is generally illiquid assets in the nature of real or personal property. Thus, a planned gift has a more restrictive definition than a major gift. However, every planned gift, by definition, is a major gift (but not the reverse) and many of them are actually outright gifts.

A deferred gift is also a type of nonrecurring gift that requires structure and design to meet the requirements of the law. While it is a planned gift, it is designed to be received at a later date. Consider for a moment that people often erroneously call all planned gifts "deferred," or vice versa, but that is not correct. Certain of these gifts that require design and structuring for legal or accounting purposes are received by the organization later and, thus, are more properly called deferred gifts. Some are designed and structured, but are outright gifts.

Looking at it from the donor's point of view once again, the donor has generally made an immediate and irrevocable transfer of funds or assets. From the donor's point of view this is anything but deferred! It is only deferred from the organization's point of view. So let us be honest; they are deferred receipts. The donor, for the most part, has made the gift. (An exception exists for revocable gifts, such as bequests, gifts within a revocable living trust or revocable remainders in a charitable remainder trust. These are not completed gifts; they are revocable deferred gifts.)

Therefore, every deferred gift is a planned gift, but not the reverse. The *gift* very well may not be deferred at all. Only the receipt is deferred.

You can see that each type of gift on the Major Gift Revenue chart is a subset of the one above it. All are, nevertheless, a form of major giving, if one is willing to step out of the development officer's shoes and stand in the shoes of the donor.

Between recurring and nonrecurring gifts there is a true, substantive difference. However, the major (nonrecurring) gifts differ only in form. That form is dictated by the donor's circumstances, not intent. If donor A has recently sold a business or gotten a large cash bonus and writes a check for $500,000, he has made an unusually large (for him) gift that will not readily recur. If donor B also makes a gift of $500,000, but transfers a parcel of real estate, that, too, is a nonrecurring gift. Donor B simply does not give that much every year or even that frequently. Both A and B made $500,000 irrevocable gifts. Donor C's circumstances are such that she can "give away the tree," but she needs to "keep the fruit" to live on. Therefore, she may put $500,000 in appreciated stock in a charitable remainder trust. All three have irrevocably parted with $500,000. Each of these three has made a major, nonrecurring gift. While the organization may book these differently, in fact, all three are major gifts that simply vary in form.

End Use of Funds

Nonprofits often use names for *revenue* programs that, in fact, indicate the end use of funds once they are obtained. For example, "capital campaign" or "endowment campaign." There is nothing inherently wrong with doing this, as long as the development professional understands what s/he is doing. Too often, new development staff are not educated as to what is revenue versus what is the end use of gifted funds. A brief nonprofit accounting course at the outset of employment as a development officer (DO) or planned gift officer (PGO) would stand the DO or PGO in good stead. In order to understand the difference between revenue generation and revenue spending, let us look at the three ways to spend gifted funds, and see how the five sources of development revenue feed into these three uses of funds.

Once you have raised money for the organization, you will soon realize that there are only three ways to use it: (1) operationally in the organization's program, (2) on capital projects or (3) by restricting it to endowment. Operational expenditures hardly need a discussion here. Nor do capital spending projects. However, endowment is poorly understood, even among fund raisers. We need to examine what endowment is as an end use and how it relates to major gifts as a revenue source. We also need to examine capital campaigns (a revenue raising tool) within the context of a major gift revenue source, and differentiate it from spending the revenue once received on capital projects. Sources and uses are two different things. Take a look at a year-end financial report. You will always see sources and uses of funds.

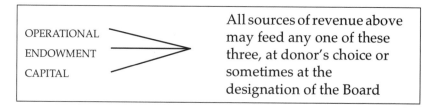

OPERATIONAL
ENDOWMENT
CAPITAL

All sources of revenue above may feed any one of these three, at donor's choice or sometimes at the designation of the Board

As an end use, there are two basic forms of endowment which must be addressed: true endowment and quasi-endowment. True endowment is restricted in a written agreement by the donor, while quasi-endowment (or funds functioning as endowment, "FFE," or board-designated endowment) is so designated by board resolution and may be changed by subsequent board resolution. These latter funds are unrestricted in accounting and legal terms. An account called "Temporary" or "Term" endowment may also exist.

True Endowment — The donor (1) restricts as to not spending the assets, (2) may restrict the use of income or other current distribution and (3) may place possible geographic, temporal or other restrictions on spending the current distribution.

Quasi-endowment — (Funds functioning as endowment) The Board designates certain funds as endowment, actually unrestricted funds in legal and accounting terms.

Endowment policies should be clearly established before funds are raised for endowment. First, the organization must pass a board resolution to create funds as endowment. Next, it must decide how to invest the funds, and finally, it must carefully express how it will spend the funds, including any assessments or charges against it for overhead.

In defining endowment, we need to realize it has centuries-long legal roots stemming from case law beginning in England hundreds of years ago and continuing to the present time. We have both case law in the U.S. courts as well as more recent legislation. The legislation is relatively new (1970s) and is contained in the Uniform Management of Institutional Funds Act. Each state decides whether or not to adopt this legislation, and each state may call it something different. The state may adopt this model legislation in whole or in part.

The legal definition from case law is that funds held as endowment when restricted by donor designation are held in "public trust." Thus, the organization's board should explicitly accept this fiduciary responsibility by passing a board resolution. The board should also have a training session as to its legal liability for not following a donor's restriction once it has promised to do so. This is, after all, money held "in trust."

The accounting definition requires that the endowment funds be kept separate from all other funds of the entity and that true endowment (that which the donor restricted to endowment as opposed to what the board voted to be endowment) be separately accounted for and not mingled with quasi-endowment or any other funds.

Funds functioning as endowment are really not "legal" endowment funds. The courts will not give them protection as to their restrictions as they do for donor-restricted endowments. Accounting standards issued by the Financial Accounting Standards Board (FASB) also require that true and quasi-endowment be kept separate. True endowment is called restricted, but quasi- or board-designated endowment is actually unrestricted money.

For centuries the courts have been very strict about upholding a donor's intent in forming or adding to an endowment. In order for an organization to change the intended use of an endowment fund, it must go to court to show that there was general charitable intent on the part of the donor and that the stated purpose is impossible or impracticable. The charity must then show that it intends to use the funds in a manner as near as possible to the original intended use. This is a very difficult standard to meet.

This type of petition to the court is called a *cy pres* action. If a state has adopted the Uniform Management of Institutional Funds Act, the state law may relax these standards by adopting a standard of inappropriateness instead of impossibility or impracticability.

The second thing an organization must do, with respect to undertaking the management and maintenance of endowment funds, is set policy as to the investment of these funds and then as to the expenditures from those funds. When determining the investment of the funds, the board must realize that the fund is designed to exist in perpetuity. It cannot be invested merely to benefit the current needs of the organization. The duty of the board is to make these funds continue on in their existence forever. A board that strips the fund in its time period of managing the nonprofit may be found to be in breach of the duties of a trustee or director of the nonprofit and, therefore, subject to fines or penalties imposed by the state Attorney General. These fines are assessed against the board member personally and are not paid by the organization. To say the least, the investment policy of an endowment fund is critical.

In addition to the concept of perpetuity, the board must determine why it is creating an endowment. If it is for a "rainy day," the investment policy may be more conservative. If it is to build funds for future program expansion, it may invest more heavily for growth, which might be inherently slightly more risky. These are decisions the board needs to make, but before it can it must be taught about endowments. Unfortunately, too few DOs and PGOs know that much about the subject, apart from hearsay.

The flip side of the coin — what to invest in to meet the stated purpose of the fund — is the amount to be spent from the fund on a yearly basis. Should only the income be spent? That is what the case law intended for centuries. However, in recent statutes, such as the Uniform Management of Institutional Funds Act, or particular state variations of it, the organization is allowed to expend some or all of the realized capital appreciation. Perhaps even unrealized capital appreciation can be distributed according to some state laws.

In states where the law permits, the spending rule adopted by the board of the organization can be based on true income as defined in the Principal and Income Act of the states' trust laws, or it may be defined as a fixed percentage of the value of the assets held by the endowment fund. It may also be a floating rate described as a range of values set forth in percentages to be multiplied by the value of the assets in the fund. If state law does not address the spending of other than actual income (dividends, interest, rents, royalties and the like) and does not expressly permit an incursion on capital growth in the fund, the organization is by law limited to the centuries-old definition of income as the amount that can and in fact must be spent (dividends, interest, rents and royalties).

In any event, whatever the intended spending rule will be, it is absolutely essential that the donor be informed in writing of the board's intended policy. Otherwise, it is logical that the donor will think that "income" (i.e., interest, dividends, etc.) only will be spent. Donors are simply not aware of these other options.

Here is a very important point to know. If promotional materials call a specific fund-raising effort an "endowment effort" or "endowment campaign," the organization has made a representation that the funds will be held in endowment and can be held to that representation by the donor's court action or by appeal to the state Attorney General. Essentially, the donee and the donor have entered into a contract of sorts, one that is called, in the law, "detrimental reliance." In other words, the donor gave funds in reliance on your promise or representation to spend it in a certain way. This is enforceable by law.

A former client called me one day somewhat upset by a call from a donor who recently responded to a mailing with a rather significant gift. The donor became concerned when he heard the DO express thanks and indicate how his gift would be spent — on a current project. The donor told him he had responded because the mailing called for endowment gifts and the organization had better make good on its representation. The DO's call to me was to ask if he had made a mistake. His rather successful mailing used the term "endowment gifts," but he really meant *major* gifts. Was he now prevented from using these new gifts on his current project? The answer is yes; he asked for endowment gifts and he made a "contract" with the donors. He could, of course, go back to each donor and ask for a written release from the endowment restriction — if state laws permitted such release. What a big mistake not to understand the difference between sources and end uses of funds.

Far too many DOs and PGOs, not to mention CEOs and CFOs, think planned gifts automatically feed into endowment. It just isn't so. Endowment and planned giving are two wildly different things — one being a restricted usage and the other being a form of revenue generation.

Let's look now at capital campaigns versus capital spending, as a revenue source. Refer back to the break down of the major gift track. If a capital campaign is planned, are its elements very different from those in this chart? What role might planned giving play?

It could serve a backup role for the donor who balks at giving a large sum outright. Perhaps s/he can give the tree, but must keep the fruit. Or, it may serve as a portion of the long-term funding plan to create a pool of funds held for ongoing maintenance and improvements for the capital asset created or refurbished in the capital campaign. See chapter 3 for a more in-depth discussion on how to coordinate planned gifts with a capital campaign and avoid unnecessary friction between the two.

Caution is advised where you have indicated or implied that funds will be used for a specific capital purpose and you have not achieved your goal. You may now want to use the funds for some other project, but the state law does not let you do that without written release from the restriction by the donor. What if you did not get a written designation of the use by the donor? What if your marketing materials "promised" to use the funds in a certain way? Can you be held to spend the money only on that project or return it to the donor? You can inadvertently create a contract or promise to spend funds on capital projects through your communications and written materials, just as for endowments as explained above. Be careful what you express in your *revenue generation* materials about the end use of funds.

2

Integrating Planned Giving into the Overall Development Effort

That which you think today becomes that which you are tomorrow.
—Napoleon Hill, *Think and Grow Rich*

The historical evolution of planned giving dates back to the founding of our country. It has had an impact on everything from the naming of Harvard and Yale Universities to the raising of money for the Community Chest during and after World War II. The birth of our current forms of charitable remainder and lead trusts, pooled income funds, gift annuities and other planned gift vehicles promoted an era of learning about planned giving. In the 1970s, charities and their advisors spent much of their time learning the then new rules imposed upon them by the Tax Reform Act of 1969.

By the 1980s, some sophistication was developing in the financial planning use of the gift vehicles. The charitable vehicles were starting to be combined with the more traditional estate planning tools to the tremendous benefit of the donor and the donee. Gift vehicles began to supplement retirement plans, be the mechanism for liquidating assets, be used in conjunction with marital deduction trusts and be combined with irrevocable life insurance trusts (to become known as wealth replacement trusts).

But the growing sophistication of financial advisors did not necessarily translate into successful planned giving programs. All over the country planned giving staff experienced the frustration of creating a successful, fruitful program while they heard wild tales of eight and nine figure gifts made to other organizations. It's like standing next to the ocean and not being able to drink.

So training courses were purchased and staff members attended to learn the complex ins and outs of tax rules facing a donor structuring a gift. But with no one for staff members to talk technically with, few gifts were happening. The solution, as it was then told in the eighties, was marketing. Marketing became a word that had to be expressed if you were in planned giving then (and now). Marketing as a word is worthless; as a practiced and understood concept, it is invaluable. In chapter 4 marketing will be discussed. (The ideas in that chapter are more fully expanded and explained in my six-audio cassette plus workbook study resource called *Marketing Magic for Major and Planned Gifts*.)

A step before marketing is to get your ducks in a row in order to make sure your new program works with and does not step on the toes of or reduce the revenue from your current fund-raising efforts. Tax rules will always be there and they will always change as soon as you learn them. They are quicksand. Good solid organization and planning are really the cornerstones of your program.

Let us start by making sure that you understand what planned giving is and is not. It is a transaction that has always been seen differently through the eyes of the donor versus the donee. From the donor's standpoint, the priorities are often pretty clear: self, family, others, including charity. The act of thinking, planning and garnering the best benefits of planned giving for these three categories is considered the "donor gift planning" aspect of planned giving. This may be done by a nonprofit staff person or by some outside source, including financial advisors, friends or neighbors, or by learning about it at a seminar. It is interesting how many people in the 1990s learn about the benefits for the family from sources other than the nonprofit development office. In fact, the role and the influence of the PGO has seriously deteriorated in this decade. However, the well-trained PGO in an organization that has taken the time to build its program's infrastructure will be highly influential both with donors and their advisors. An ineffectual PGO or planned gift program will be bypassed by a planner instead of seen as a resource.

The donee's perspective should be that planned giving is a programmatic effort, a consistent *effort* to develop gifts that are "structured," more significant in size than those recurring annually and designed to meet a donor's needs and objectives. This programmatic effort includes the planning, marketing and delivery of appropriate gift structures and vehicles through a Planned Gift Program.

By now you should see that the planned gift program is indeed more than the sum of its vehicles. The vehicles are simply the devices that get a donor's money or assets from his or her pocket to the donee's in the best manner for at least the donor and family, if not also the donee.

It is important to realize the planned gift program is an ongoing, evolutionary process rather than an event. Setting up the program and then gift planning and structuring for a donor takes time, structure, commitment and funding to succeed. The creation of the program is, therefore, an *entrepreneurial* undertaking. What does that mean? How long does it take to start a new business? How long until it is profitable?

I have often asked board members to whom I am making an initial presentation on adopting a planned gift program if any have created their own businesses. Generally, at least one has done so. I ask if they are willing to share their story of success. Specifically, I ask if they were profitable right away or whether it took some time to turn the red ink into black, and if so, how long it took.

The responses I have received have been precious and moving. Some of them have gone bankrupt or nearly so before they turned the corner. They have experienced the joy and the sorrow of starting-up a business. Each story told has its own tale of strength that the other board members get to hear. When the person is finished speaking, and often they take the time to tell their story, the board understands that this was not an overnight success. One fellow clearly outlined his seven year struggle to make his company profitable. I promised that it would not take that long for planned giving *if* they were serious about putting into it the same effort and commitment that this man did with his business. But all parties must realize that this is, really and truly, the startup of a new business. It takes the same amount of effort and attention. The person assigned to carry it out must have the ability to pursue it regularly, if not full time.

Let us take a look at your starting point. Every organization is different: different board, different community, different purpose, different length of existence, different initial or endowment funding and on and on. So how can we generalize about determining where to start? The very first thing to do is assess what you already have. This might result in having to face some hard truths. Perhaps there are other organizational things that need to be done before you can undertake planned giving. Remember that planned giving is not a panacea for lack of successful fund raising.

One organization sent its development person to see me in my office to discuss setting up a planned gift program. She told me they *had* to do this right now. I asked why, did they have a substantial gift pending that they did not want to miss? Oh no, she replied, it was quite the opposite. They needed to get gifts, and get them soon, because they were in dire financial straits. I asked about the possible deferred nature of many planned gifts. Well, she had heard that they would get *big* gifts through planned giving, that is what she was after. Unfortunately, her organization was large and should have been sophisticated. I had to tell her the hard truth that management needed to get healthy, because no one would commit large dollars long-term to a sinking ship.

So let us begin the assessment with your current fund-raising effort. Then we will move to determining the extent of the program you wish to adopt. Third, we will look at how to avoid friction points and snags in the process. And lastly, we will look at who will manage the function on a daily basis. Once this is done, we can move to the planning stage to create business and marketing plans. Then, all we have to do is just do it.

Four Steps to Integration

Step One

There are four basic steps to integrating a planned gift program. Step one involves assessing your organization's readiness to undertake planned giving. Within this first step are three primary areas of concern regarding readiness: (1) examining the internal staffing and working structure of the development office, (2) tracing and targeting gift history and donor records and (3) analyzing other internal and external capabilities and / or weaknesses.

Because tracing and targeting gifts and records involves the basis for developing pools of prospects for one type of marketing technique, we will look at this concern in chapter 4. For now, let's look at the other two concerns.

In examining the internal structure of the development office, consider how the five parts of the development office chart fit into your organization. Are there specific plans and programs that are written out and approached in an orderly manner? Or, is your development office just a hodge-podge of activities? In other words, from day to day does the staff (maybe that is you) run frantically from one thing to another without the time or ability or direction to move systematically forward on one or more projects you hope to achieve? Be honest. More offices than you think are engaged in frantic running from thing to thing. We need to go back to Yogi Berra, who said something like, if you don't know where you are going, it may be very hard to get there. Your office needs to be brought into order; it cannot be careening from hither to yon and think it can develop a planned gift effort. This effort needs to be as well planned and as systematic as a capital campaign.

Assuming the office is fairly well organized in what it does up to this point, the next question is whether it is a one-person or a multi-staffed development effort. Look back at the Development Office chart. Is there separate staff for each type of revenue source? If not, do staff members, whether one or more, have separate time allocated exclusively for each task assigned? Is there a separate budget for each type of revenue source? A planned gift effort requires a lot of time and activity in a continuous fashion as you will see when we get into an analysis of task detailing on a time study basis. If your office is not accustomed to allocating time to separate activities and respecting that time allocation faithfully, some discipline will need to be developed and adhered to. I have had success with time allocation even in somewhat chaotic circumstances if there is another desk or office that the DO assigned to planned giving can go to at least one day a week *faithfully* without being dragged away for other more important things, like blowing up balloons for the special event dinner tonight or making out invitations for the golf tournament. No discipline, no planned gifts. I guarantee it.

If you have the luxury of hiring a planned giving person exclusively for the new program from the outset, this may not be such a concern. In reality, few organizations start by hiring a full or part-time staff person devoted to planned giving. If you do have that luxury, the next question is whether this person about to become your PGO has ever started a program from scratch. Most have not. They have worked in an ongoing program and were assigned to do certain tasks. The chance that they know how to create one is slim. So, if that is the case, and that is the person you have already hired, be concerned about how creative and resourceful s/he is. Resourcefulness can overcome a lack of know-how. Also, if your type of industry is different from the type of industry in which your new PGO has experience, such as a hospital hiring someone from a university setting, you may have difficulties. See the chapter on marketing. A university has a built-in, closed marketing system for the most part. A hospital or true charity does not. The techniques learned at the former organization may fall flat on their faces when transposed. So be sure to ask these questions at the outset. Your best bet for the PGO may very well be someone right in the development office who has a firm grasp of the basic fund-raising principles and an entrepreneurial spirit. Do not overlook him or her due to a lack of technical background. Technical expertise can be purchased; spirit, discipline, cooperation and an understanding of the organization will far outweigh a technical person's knowledge with none of these other attributes.

On the subject of staffing, how does the office use its volunteers? If you follow the method in this book, you will find you have too many prospects to handle. The role of volunteers in planned giving has many contenders. Some nonprofits use them wisely and achieve amazing results financially, while others abuse them by making them attend endless committee meetings for no purpose. In chapter 5, the use of committees will be discussed. But, at this point you should know that you may need to learn to use volunteers so as not to waste valuable leads you have turned up, some of whom may be expecting a call or some information from you. If you cannot respond because you are too busy, forget ever going back to that prospect. You have just trashed a prospect.

A very important point, and one never to be overlooked in the early stages, is that the activities of creating the program may appear to the short-term funding mentality to be signs of inactivity or just diddling around. This program honestly takes some time and planning effort while sitting at a desk for a little while. I have known many PGOs who get caught in this phase endlessly because they do not know what to do next, and, after all, chasing tax law is kind of fun. Not surprisingly, it does not bring in gifts. Nevertheless, at the outset, there is written work and meetings that must be accomplished.

This first area of concern, with respect to readiness, is about whether the development office, as it currently exists, can really carry it off or whether it needs to stop and pull itself together before trying a new program. Hard truths. Please be honest when you make this assessment and do it in writing. Ask yourself the following questions:

(1) Of the five sources of revenue, how many are we now actively pursuing?

(2) Of each that we are pursuing, what is the success of each one?

(3) Which staff person and how much time each week is absolutely dedicated to each source of revenue?

(4)   Do we have someone who knows, not planned giving or gift vehicles, but how to *create* a new planned gift *program*?

(5)   How do we use volunteers and can we use them in planned giving?

(6)   Will others allow the person assigned to planned giving to do his/her tasks without interruption?

(7)   Do we have someone in-house who can do this?

(8)   Do we have budget allocated for this? (See the chapter on business plans.)

(9)   Is office space available?

(10)   Is support staff available to help at least part-time without fail?

(11)   Is there an ability and willingness to change cultivation techniques and intake procedures?

Write out your answers and discuss them internally, do not put them in a desk drawer. If you uncover a problem, work to resolve it. Remember this is a threshold to creating a solid new program.

Now let us move on to the third concern regarding readiness. (Remember the second will be discussed in the marketing chapter.)

Up to this point we have focused on the development office itself. We must now move outward and assess the other parts of the organization that must be helpful and supportive to make the program work. Not everyone knows about your program or frankly cares if it is a success. You will need to sell them on its merits. After that we will look beyond the organization and into the community.

In terms of an organization's realistic capabilities, let us think internally first. Which office will handle funds administration for planned gifts? This office will need to work with you in a spirit of cooperation. Not to be negative, but over the many years that I have served as a consultant to various organizations, this has proven to be a challenge. Apathetic or even hostile attitudes can be encountered at first. If you do not have this problem, consider yourself and your organization blessed. More often it is merely apathy and a view that the office that has been processing gifts all along can do this thing called planned giving, too. No problem. That is until a problem is faced and it usually involves an antici-pated, missed or wrong payment to a donor or other beneficiary. The donor has only had contact with the development office, so if it is not working right, after the gift is closed, guess who gets the upset phone call.

Again, not to be negative, but for the most part, the staff per-sons assigned to processing gifts do not usually interface with the donors and do not usually know about donor relations. So the problem can quickly compound if the development officer does not step in. What if the development officer did not bother to learn what to do after the gift is closed because that is "someone else's job?"

As for the staff person who handles funds, his or her perspec-tive is just the opposite. That person may feel that this new load has been dumped on him or her in addition to everything else, and on top of it all s/he has no training in these new gift vehicles.

I had an interesting experience with a multiple-campus statewide university system I worked with on a regular basis. Of course, I worked with the development staff. I was asked to meet with the funds administrators for a day-long training session on how to handle planned gift processing and crediting. At the be-ginning of the meeting I asked each of the representatives of the various campuses (about twenty-five attendees in all) to say who they were, how they got involved in dealing with planned gifts and what they thought of it. Well, an hour and a half later, after having one colossal gripe session on planned giving departments, we started my planned itinerary.

That first hour and a half, however, gave me tremendous in-sight into the frustrations of the funds administration officer. Each of them reported that they had no idea what these vehicles actual-ly were, how they worked and, most of all, why a donor would choose one over another in the form they did. They could not put their work in context, therefore, they could not really understand it. Whereas I mostly planned to talk about processing and detail, we carved out a good portion of time to satisfy their curiosity about donor gift structuring. Once they had the chance to see the excitement of planned gift structuring, I could see they would be the very best allies a PGO could ever want in an organization.

Whose job is it to train the funds administrator? Do you know of any really good courses for them? For this reason, I developed a course, *After the Gift is Closed*. I believe that no matter what course you or they go to, the DO and the funds administrator should attend together. Right then and there you can resolve almost all of your problems and close the gaps. All too often, however, I hear from the DO, "That is not what I do. I do not need that course." Or, "We do not serve as trustee, so I do not need that course." This latter comment is the height of misunderstanding about the role of the DO in the planned gift process. "It's not my job" will not suffice in this arena. Ask yourself these questions about your funds administration staff:

(1)   Is there a willingness to learn new procedures?
(2)   Are there written procedures currently developed for processing planned gifts?
(3)   Is there an ability to add/train staff?
(4)   Is there a willingness to coordinate with the DO during the negotiation and gift structure process?
(5)   Is there a willingness to think "yes" rather than "no?"

What will you do if the answer to these questions is negative? Will there be support higher up? These are essential to the equation. Write out your answers and share the report with your next immediate supervisor to work out the problems. Please actually do this exercise. It will save you costly errors and badwill later.

Let us move to public relations. If you have an in-house public relations staff, and you must use that staff, you also need to assess its strengths and its willingness to work with you. Sometimes, PR work with respect to the program elements (not fund raising) seems to be the priority or even the sole job of the PR department. Any fund-raising work is a low priority and any other deadline will overrule. If this attitude exists, it needs to be corrected quickly. It generally takes someone above both of you to sort out priorities. Once in a while, this office needs to know what percentage of the total revenue of the organization comes from fund raising, and, therefore, what percentage of that staff's salary is represented by the work you do. Use your net figures from chapter 1 if you absolutely need to make this point. When creating your integration effort, ask the following questions:

(1)   Is there a willingness to give full support to your program?

(2)   Is there a willingness to learn where the money comes from?

(3)   Is there a compatibility or ability to work jointly with the development office?

(4)   Is there a willingness to include planned giving deadlines in their timeline?

(5)   Is there an ability to accept changes necessary to incorporating technical information or accept your way of expressing it without ego involvement and struggles?

Write out your responses honestly and discuss any problems with your supervisor.

Last, but not least, is your board and your CEO. I have found very few CEOs who will sit still for very long for any presentation on planned giving unless they worked in the development business themselves at one time. As to the overall development program, they must commit time, but as to one aspect of the development effort, that is a different question. Should the CEO spend the time to hear you out on planned giving? Why not on special events or annual giving? At the outset, the CEO must absolutely understand what you are proposing and buy into it. Perhaps the best way to get that to happen is to have a board member take up the cause for you. Often the board is involved in planned giving in other organizations and may be anxious to get it going in your shop, too. What the organization is undertaking is a fiduciary role; that means it will be guarding and preserving the assets of another. That entails specific legal duties that expose the CEO and the board to significant risk of breach of that fiduciary duty. You will have confidential financial information. You may be involved in the tax and financial plans of the donor or the handling of large sums of money. You may be obligated to buy, sell or invest on behalf of an individual or individuals who are counting on you. You may have made representations and promises, to those individuals, for which the organization and its board and management can be sued. Is that serious enough for the CEO to stop and take notice? Probably. Be careful how you express this, however. If it is too scary, you may end up with no program. Ask these questions at a minimum:

(1) Does the CEO and the board understand the "what" and "why" of the undertaking?

(2) Are they willing and able to do long-range planning that includes this effort?

(3) Are they, and especially the CEO, willing to delegate to the development office the contact with the largest donors and not maintain a "Mom and Pop Grocery Store" style of control over fund raising for the important donor?

(4) Will they devote some time to this?

(5) Can they stomach the cultivation period without revenue from the program and not keep asking you where the money is?

(6) Will they understand that the projections you made are just that — projections — and not dollar goals and that you cannot predict when life beneficiaries will die?

(7) Is there a willingness to measure *goals* in other than dollar terms, at least for the first several years?

Write out your responses. Who do you share these answers with? First, your supervisor, but secondly a trusted board member if you have one. This one can be tough. A recalcitrant CEO or board chair may indicate that you should look elsewhere for greener pastures. Often the CEO wall avidly state that s/he wants a planned giving program, but when it comes time to get involved, s/he really just wants someone else to do it and magically get results.

Once you have honestly analyzed your internal organization and ferreted out, and hopefully resolved, any problems, you need to consider your image in, and relationship with, the community. Community needs defining here. It can be geographic if yours is a geographic-based organization. Or it can be a community of interest, like Ducks Unlimited or Experimental Aircraft Association Aviation Foundation, which extends nationwide for people of common interests. If your relationship with your community is tarnished, you will indeed have a hard time obtaining large commitments of funds and assets. In fact, I have seen organizations hit the newspapers for very minor problems that result in very major impediments to the long-term commitment required of the planned gift donor. Ask yourself these questions:

(1) Does your organization have a good image in the community?
(2) Has it recently had any publicity problems?
(3) Does your organization have good connections in the financial community, or an ability to form new relationships with the outside world?
(4) Is there a willingness to learn how to function as a partner with attorneys, CPAs, CLUs (insurance), CFPs (financial planning), trust officers, investment officers, real estate brokers, etc.?

Once again, write out your responses and review them with your supervisor to forestall any problems.

There were five exercises in step one requiring written responses and subsequent staff meetings and discussions. If you will take the time to do these exercises, you will have a good start at effective integration.

Step Two

The second step of integration involves understanding the planned giving program (i.e., the elements of the effort on a consistent basis) to the point that it can more smoothly blend into an organization's current effort. Again, a planned giving program is more than the sum of its vehicles. It is the consistent and overall effort to identify and bring prospective donors to the organization; to use life income gifts and gift structuring to the fullest advantage of both the donor and the donee; and to organize, manage and implement staff and volunteer efforts to bring gifts of a sophisticated nature to fruition in support of the long-term goals of the organization.

In further understanding the program, examine what could cause tensions, problems and concerns in your organization. The following list consists of items that have caused concern to others in varying degrees. You and others in the organization need to come to grips with these thoughts:

- Is this fund raising or is it financial planning? If it is financial planning, are you engaged in something improper for an organization to do?
- Is there a specific set of ethics that should pertain to your dealings with the donor public?
- To what degree are we responsible to know and convey to the donor matters of a technical nature relating to the gift?
- Because this is a highly personalized, long-term form of fund raising with close contact, will we be accused of undue influence?
- Significant planning and strategizing is required — in house, with volunteers and with donors. Are we competent to do it?
- There is a constant need to educate and then to update staff members. Are we willing to undertake it and pay for it on a regular basis?
- To what degree are we willing to do gift planning in depth per donor versus sending the donor out to other advisors?
- Are we ready for new types of record-keeping and reports?
- Are we aware of and do we accept new liabilities, e.g. fiduciary responsibility?

All of these things are necessary parts of a planned giving program, just as necessary as gift vehicles and tax consequences. You do not want to find yourself in the middle of these issues accidentally. You definitely want to think them through and prepare for them before opening the doors for business. No new business would start up (or would succeed) without having its systems in place. Write out your answers and think these through. Many of these items will turn up again in board policies in chapter 5.

In addition, there will be all the ideas and written materials required in the chapters covering the business plan, the marketing plan and ethics. Together these form the basis of your organization's understanding of where it is going with planned giving.

Step Three

Step three involves an assessment of potential friction points. Internal friction or competitiveness and territorial tendencies can carry over into communications with donors, who are inclined to notice such things.

Think for a moment about how this friction might impact annual giving. Here are some issues to consider:

(1) Annual giving staff may feel that pursuing a planned gift program may eliminate the donor's annual gift. How does the donor see it? What is the approach? (See resolution below.)

(2) Consider the opposite view: highly personalized, long-term planned giving cultivation increases a donor's awareness of organizational needs, drawing the donor closer to the organization. The donor becomes a "shareholder" in the organization via a planned gift and looks after his/her "investment."

(3) Both annual and planned gift staff should realize the importance of recognizing the need for annual operating funds and communicate that to the donor.

(4) Avoid the double ask of recurring and nonrecurring programs by working together in four coordinating strategies (see below).

(5) Avoid territoriality, resentment and misunderstanding of colleagues. Planned giving is not "better" or "superior." It is fund raising. It is necessary for long-

term institutional viability and it should be reported to the development director and be part of the team.

(6)   Planned, but not deferred, gifts may be partially or wholly credited to the annual fund. Deferred gifts may use one of four strategies below.

(7)   Life insurance gifts may be structured to pull out cash value each year for operating fund while receiving death proceeds as a deferred gift.

There are four ways that your deferred gifts can augment your current coffers:

(1)   Once you have worked with the donor to determine that s/he has low yielding assets that can be repositioned for a higher payout, consider asking him/her if s/he could share some of the newfound **income** with your organization by writing into the trust agreement a share — say five to ten percent — payable directly to the organization each year for the duration of the trust. For example, if the donor was receiving a two percent return on his or her assets and will now receive a seven percent return from a CRT or gift annuity, perhaps 0.7 percent could be paid to you. This leaves 6.3 percent for the beneficiary, still more than three times what s/he was receiving.

(2)   Another possibility is to ask the donor to split the **asset** and give the organization directly a five to ten percent share as an outright gift. This achieves the same return for the donor as in number one above, but the organization has its share up front.

(3)   If a definite share of income is not possible, consider having the donor allow the trustee the discretion to distribute some income to the organization in years where the earnings are sufficient. This does not absorb income each and every year.

(4)   If a definite share of the **asset** is not available, perhaps the trustee could be given discretion to invade the principal for distributions to the organization if the trust's

asset value grows beyond a certain amount, such as greater than 150 percent of the original contributed amount.

If none of these are available to lock into the trust agreement itself, the beneficiary could decide to relinquish a portion of the income interest at a later date, which allows the trustee to distribute some principal at that time.

As explained in chapter 1, the difference from the donor's perspective between planned and major gifts is one of form only, not substance. To the donor, it *is* a major gift.

Now think for a moment how internal friction might impact a major gifts program and consider these issues:

(1)   Use of same lists — need for coordination.
(2)   Use of same volunteers — need for coordination.
(3)   Planned giving as fall back position for major gift staff where gift is otherwise lost.
(4)   Planned gifts officer as support staff to major gifts. Is planned giving really a separate program? Should all major gift officers be planned giving officers? Think through the best major gift/planned gift organizational structure on an institution by institution basis. No one answer is perfect for all organizations.

Now think about its potential impact on a capital campaign, or vice versa. Consider these issues:

(1)   Capital campaign consultants sometimes wish to suspend deferred giving solicitation and possibly planned gift solicitation (other than those planned gifts countable toward the campaign immediately, such as gifts of closely-held stock or real estate).
(2)   The capital campaign machinery is usable to planned giving on an ongoing basis once the campaign is over.
        — Prospect identification
        — Research
        — Volunteer structure

— Time frame/pressure/motivation
— Very clear case
— More money permitted as cost of
   fund raising
— May be connected with long-term
   planning

(3)   The whole organization must realize that capital cam-
      paign is only a major gift/planned gift effort on a dif-
      ferent time frame.

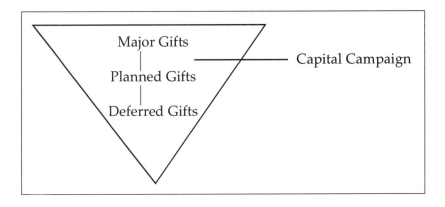

(4)   There should be an organizational effort to sustain the
      characteristics of the campaign for ongoing, long-term
      benefit. (See number two above.)

(5)   The organization needs to address campaign crediting
      and counting of *deferred* dollars, revocable and irrevoca-
      ble. If it is truly a *capital* campaign, i.e. building, plant
      and capital needs, then a portion of that need is clearly
      long-term and may need funds that come in later to
      keep pace with the cost. Many campaign consultants
      now assign a specified dollar portion to endowing the
      building. This can be fulfilled with planned gifts. Ques-
      tion: What credit will the donor receive, face or actuari-
      al value? Is there an alternative? Most organizations
      and the recent accounting (FASB) standards suggest

use of actuarial remainder value for booking a gift. Consider whether campaign credit could be different than financial reporting.

(6)   The planned giving staff should be included in every campaign strategy / prospect meeting. How can you activate your listening strategy?

(7)   When can planned giving give the campaign a "shot in the arm."

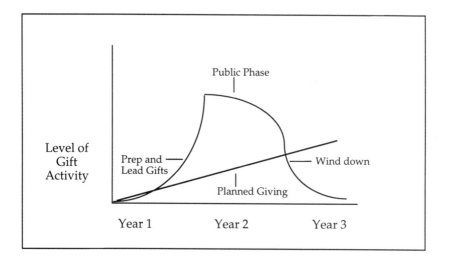

(8)   Timeline of the Campaign: The preparation stage and the lead gifts can take the better part of a year. After the decided-upon lead gifts are secured, the public portion of the campaign is announced. Somewhere in the middle to the end of the campaign, gift levels and activity start to fall off. At a certain point, perhaps two years into a three-year campaign, efforts to raise funds may get more difficult.

Planning for the widespread entry of planned gifts into the campaign should begin early in the campaign in preparation for that period. Planned giving can then serve an important function in picking up during a slack time and maybe even save the campaign.

The results are beneficial to both the campaign and to the planned giving program, which benefits from the structure and discipline of the campaign. It can then "leap-frog" off the campaign into a much higher level of sustained activity. (Or it can be the beginning of a planned gift program if none existed before the campaign.) The planned giving leap-frog can also save the day in the slump period right after a campaign.

(9)   Here is an example of appropriate use of a planned gift in a capital campaign:

A sixty year-old female architect has real estate worth $500,000, based on $100,000 as a significant asset, but a small pension plan and not a lot of income ($70,000 per year). She is on the board of a children's home and they have asked her for a campaign gift. She is widowed and has two children and has stated that her only major asset is reserved for their inheritance. While she would like to make a gift, she feels that she can only afford $5,000 out of her current savings. After discussing it with her, you may suggest a planned gift. She needs the following if she is to make a planned gift: income from assets in retirement, a current deduction, an immediate gift to two children for their needs for down payments on homes, ultimate gifts to children via her estate and a significant gift to charity's capital campaign currently. The property is not mortgaged, and no accelerated depreciation has been taken.

Real Estate

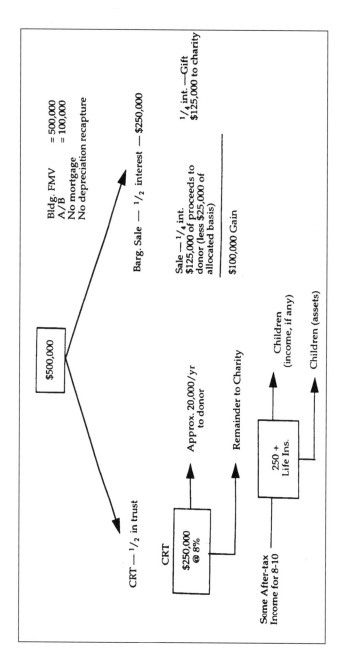

Bldg. FMV = 500,000
A/B = 100,000
No mortgage
No depreciation recapture

Barg. Sale — $^1/_2$ interest — $250,000

$^1/_4$ int. —Gift
$125,000 to charity

Sale — $^1/_4$ int.
$125,000 of proceeds to
donor (less $25,000 of
allocated basis)

$100,000 Gain

$500,000

CRT — $^1/_2$ in trust

CRT

$250,000
@ 8%

Approx. 20,000/yr
to donor

Remainder to Charity

Children
(income, if any)

Children (assets)

Some After-tax
Income for 8-10

250 +
Life Ins.

(1) Deductions: From CRT, $70,000; from Bargain Sale, $125,000; total deduction of $195,000
(2) Gain: $100,000 includible vs. $195,000 deductible; net deduction of $95,000; caution percentage limitations and AMT
(3) Children: Current gifts of $62,500 each for down payments
(4) Donor: Increased income, later even more; deductions; gifts to kids; gifts to charity
(5) Charity: Two gifts—$125,000 now, trusts later.

You will see from this case that one asset can be used for many purposes, both family and charity. Here, what we have accomplished is to split the property, to benefit Mom in retirement, and replace this amount with life insurance for the children's inheritance and place the remainder interest in the trust as a future gift. That part is accomplished while still achieving an immediate outright gift for the children in the amount of $62,500 for down payments for homes for each of them, and for the charity in the amount of $125,000 for the campaign. The result is that all of Mom's stated needs and wants are met. At the outset she thought she could only afford a $5,000 gift in her circumstances. Instead, she gave $125,000 to the campaign, along with a trust now worth $250,000. She will have retirement income when she retires in eight years, and the children have an advance on their inheritance, in addition to the life insurance and any other assets Mom leaves to them by will or living trust.

This should show you how planned/deferred gifts can and should fit, not cause friction, in the campaign.

Step Four

The fourth step in integrating a planned giving program involves an organization's ability to manage the planned giving function once it is in place.

Management of this function requires considerable attention on the part of staff members. If the program relies on a part-time person, focused time is essential. Can the organization afford it? Will it permit it? Or will the planned giving person be pulled from his/her job for every unusual need, such as setting forks around tables for special events, or helping put labels on last-minute mailings? This is not to say these aren't necessary tasks. However, be sure there are not so many that the planned gift work does not get accomplished. In a one-person or two-person development office, there is always something that must be done on a crisis basis and planned giving keeps getting pushed farther and farther back. The DO may simply not know what to do next.

Unfortunately, when other more immediate matters need

constant attention, the in-office activities of organization, preparation, implementation and ongoing management of a planned gift program are often mistaken by others as inactivity, especially when placed in an environment of short-term goals and fund-raising cycles.

This impression needs to be corrected (or avoided) through approval of a twelve-month chronology and use of it as the evaluation tool. Also, specifically, the signed Board Treaty, which we will introduce later, is very helpful in this regard.

Education and updates are crucial to the program. Incorrect or outdated advice will cause tremendous donor relations problems. In many cases, donors, and their advisors, will rely on the planned giving office. You cannot let them down. However, this requires time away from the office and money spent on staff education. Is the organization ready to accept that?

The choice of planned giving personnel is also critical. *Longevity* is one of the primary keys to a successful program, as described in the introduction. Donors come to trust the staff person over the years.

Turnover is a severe setback to a planned giving program in the one-person development office, the one-person planned giving office and even, to a great degree, in a multiple-staffed office where the person in question has sole contact with a group of donors.

With that said, the organization — from top down — must exert itself to provide an atmosphere conducive to personnel retention. It must also determine the scope and visibility of the program, which will depend upon time, budget, constituency and competition. It will revolve around what vehicles will be used, and to what degree the organization involves itself in the program's promotion. How much public visibility is desired is a question that should be settled early.

The organization must then determine its willingness to train volunteers. Volunteers should be included in the program for different types of tasks. They must understand the nature of the program, the types of gift vehicles and the donor situations in which such vehicles are useful. Because volunteers turn over, the organization must also be willing to have continual training efforts. See the chapter on Working Effectively Within Your Organization for a discussion of using volunteers in planned giving.

Should Planned Gift Recognition Be Different from Other Types

Let's consider this idea using some common sense scenarios. The donor of a planned gift is likely to see him/herself as a "shareholder" of the institution. Committing long-term funds will (should) mean long-term involvement by a donor. When a donor parts with $50,000 or $500,000, s/he never really parts with it because s/he always wants to know what is happening with "my money."

Recognition, therefore, must track the ownership concept. Special parties, plaques, the naming of rooms and other recognition events can, will and should evoke in *others* the donor's ownership stake.

Consider now both the donor's and the organization's commitment to a community. A community may be a town or city, it may be grateful patients or an alumni body or it may be a commonality of interest among members. In any case, a planned gift donor has made a long-term commitment to that community. Recognition must reflect the nature and extent of the community and the community's thanks for such commitment. The commitment here can be money or time.

Let's look at some modes of recognition. First, private and in-depth contact:

- Board Chairman or key board member makes personal visit or takes donor to lunch/dinner/cocktails as a thank you
- Staff and/or Planned Giving Volunteer Committee makes *periodic* (on a tickler file) thank-you lunch or visit — no solicitation

- Send birthday cards, Christmas or Hanukkah cards
- Other, such as joining in help the elderly programs; helping donor with trips to friends, doctors, grocery stores; organizing outings to parks, museums, etc.
- Premiums — art objects, books, etc. as gifts to donor

Here are some other more public modes of recognition:

(1)   Annual dinners
(2)   Listings in newsletters (or full articles)
(3)   Use in case studies for seminars
(4)   Reading a case study at a seminar
(5)   News media where appropriate
(6)   Scheduled donor activities: meetings, letters, privileges at the institution, public affairs forums on issues of interest, field trips, tours, etc.
(7)   Recruitment for Board, Committees
(8)   Advisory Group to executive regarding special projects, issues (giving them a real voice in the matter).

The answer, then, is a hearty yes. Recognition is different with planned gifts, not only because of the high level of gifts but because of the long-term faith (or investment) each donor shows in the organization. It might help to think of this concept as "Shareholder Giving."

SECTION TWO

"PLAN"

When schemes are laid in advance, it is surprising how often circumstances fit in with them.

— Sir William Osler

3

Developing A Business Plan That Works

Money is the seed of money, and the first guinea is sometimes more difficult to acquire than the second million.

— Jean Jacques Rousseau
The International Thesaurus of Quotations
by Rhoda Thomas Tripp

In the introduction of this book, we compared the launching of a planned giving program to that of starting a business. Just like opening a shoe store, it starts with a plan. In researching and building the business plan, however, we must also keep in mind the end result; the payoff.

It's the plan that leads us to that end, the plan that helps us determine our revenue projections, expected expenses, the size and scope of our program, the chronological steps that will lead to its implementation and a set of evaluations which will keep our program running smoothly and effectively. Those are the ingredients of a well-developed business plan, a business plan that works.

Let's delve into these areas, outlining an approach to and expected result of each task. In seeking revenue projections, what better place to start our research than with a comparative study of similarly situated organizations who have adopted and are successfully operating a planned giving program.

Organizations generally have revenue from fund-raising programs, such as annual gifts or major gifts, before they undertake a planned gift program. Often those programs have been in place for a considerable length of time. When the organization feels that it can sustain trust and estate gifts, it entertains the idea of a planned giving program. The nature of the gift in a planned gift program is complex and involves transfers of money or property for annuities or in trust, or gifts of real estate or closely-held or restricted stock, or one of many other types of gifts requiring legal or accounting structure. This is generally quite different from what the organization has already engaged in.

To ensure that the decision to spend the funds on the new program is prudent, the board and the staff should prepare a business plan as if the organization were borrowing from a bank to fund this new program. If it can successfully prepare such a business plan, not only will the decision to expend the funds for the new planned giving program be wisely made, but the basic blueprint for the new program will have been drafted.

Fund raising — encouraging transfers of money and property from "detached and disinterested generosity" as the tax court cases call it — is not the same as a business because it depends upon a person's inclination and decision to make a substantial gift, one far greater than s/he would ordinarily make yearly. Thus, it is important to use the best of the thoughts from the business world, tempered with the reality of the fund-raising world.

A business plan for planned giving will be made in four parts: (1) a description of the "product," (2) a projection of revenue to be earned over a given period of time, (3) an analysis of likely expenses over the same time period and (4) a chronology of activities to achieve the proposed revenue.

Over the time period of the plan, the potential yield on the assets invested in this program by the organization may be calculated. Because many fund-raising programs have *goals* to meet each year, it is important to understand that these projected revenues and yields are just that — projections for planning purposes, not promises. Revenue projections and fund-raising goals are two different things.

The "Product" Of Planned Giving

Clearly, the organization starting its planned giving program will need to determine just what vehicles it intends to use at the outset. Many organizations ask why they cannot start with all of them. Some can, but just as with anything else in life, it is better to do some things very well rather than try to do all things and do none well. Every gift vehicle requires time, money and effort to put it in place and then to market it vigorously to achieve success.

In chapter 1 we examined many sources of revenue and development programs that help to achieve it. Now you must look at each specific tool to be used in the planned giving program in terms of the TIME, available MARKET, staff's KNOWLEDGE, the organization's COST and the TASKS REQUIRED to achieve revenue from that vehicle.

Looking at the adoption of gift vehicles, or "product" if this were a for-profit business plan, in terms of time, money committed, potential market and knowledge required of staff and volunteers will help you determine which ones you can really undertake and in what time frame.

The lowest level in terms of time, money and knowledge, while appeal is made to the overall market, is:

- Bequests
- Life insurance

The second level of the program, depending upon staff time, money and knowledge, while still appealing to a broad market, is:

- Pooled income fund
- Charitable gift annuities
- Deferred gift annuities

The third level requiring more staff time, money and knowledge while appealing to targeted markets rather than the whole market is:

- Annuity trusts
- Unitrusts
- Life estates and remainder interest in residences and farm

Fourth and top level in terms of time, money and especially knowledge while the vehicles appeal specifically to target markets (but they often produce high-dollar volume from a small number of gifts from those markets) is:

- Unitrusts in the form of net-income with makeup or flip unitrusts, with their many applications
- Unitrusts to be invested for total return
- Unitrusts for diversification of assets
- Charitable remainder trusts as retirement vehicles
- Charitable lead trusts
- Remainders in exchange for annuities
- Real estate in general
- Complex gifts of tangible personal and intangible property (such as partnership interests, oil and gas leases, closely-held securities, etc.)
- Transfer of "fancy assets" (patents, copyrights, franchises, claims, settlements, etc.)

The above four levels imply continual and consistent effort to market these vehicles and to attract donor interest in these vehicles. You need not adopt the gift vehicles in the order presented here and, in fact, your market may require that you jump into more difficult ones early on. You simply need to be sure that you can *handle* the ones selected.

Revenue Projections

At the outset of a planned gift program, it is always difficult to establish revenue projections because the type of gift relies on circumstances beyond our control — i.e., when a person will do his/her estate planning or when s/he will die. Therefore, it is necessary to build projections based on the experience of other successful organizations in conjunction with the organization's own experience in its fund-raising program. The following four parts of the revenue projection should give you some firm ground to stand on when projecting revenue for the new program for the next few years.

Comparative Survey

First, you should undertake a comparative survey of organizations that are similarly situated and that have had a planned giving program for three to five years or even more. Most organizations will be very willing to share their information. Your best method of comparison is, once you have received responses to your questions, put them in grid or matrix form so that you can see the comparison at a glance. In order to make a valid comparison of the results of other organizations to your organization, you will need to come to the understanding that certain organizations are, in fact, similarly situated to yours. The process of selecting similarly-situated organizations will be critical to the success of this process.

The selection of similarly situated organizations must be based on organizations having characteristics that lead to similar results in marketing the fund-raising effort. For example: (1) the organization must have a similar constituency in size and wealth, (2) the organization must be similarly organized, such as religious affiliation, part of a chain, local, regional or national, etc., (3) the organization must exist in a community that can be defined as similar to your organization's community (size, heavy retirement area, state of economy, near large urban area, ethnic mix, etc.), (4) the competition for the fund-raising dollar should be about the same, (5) the image of the organization should be approximately the same and (6) if your organization has any strong specialty or uniqueness, then the compared organizations should have either a similar uniqueness, or at least a uniqueness of another kind that is comparable. You should start your search for these through your professional associations, such as National Committee for Planned Giving, American Council on Gift Annuities, National Society for Fund Raising Executives, Association for Health Care Philanthropy, Council for the Support and Advancement of Education, National Association of College and University Business Officers and others. You may also wish to put a message on the Internet to ask for responses.

What do you ask the similarly situated organizations once you find them? The information you are soliciting is that which will give you an idea of your potential for raising revenue through planned giving. Some questions you may wish to pose include:

(1)   What were their budgets for the first three to five years of their programs?

(2)   What planned gift vehicles were selected to be marketed?

(3)   What markets were approached?

(4)   What marketing methods were employed?

(5)   What were their annual gift revenues for the same number of years?

(6)   If they kept separate records for major gifts and planned gifts, what were their major gift results for those years?

(7)   How many bequest intentions did they receive in those years?

(8)   How much did they receive in matured bequests in those years?

(9)   How many planned gifts were closed (not distributions received) per year for the first three to five years? If they are willing to do more work, you may request that they break these down into dollar amounts per type of gift vehicle.

(10)   What actual revenue distributions occurred from these gift vehicles during the first three to five years? Either in the aggregate or by gift vehicle.

(11)   How many part- or full-time staff persons work on planned gifts?

(12)   If they were starting over, what would they do differently?

This is best reported to management and the board on a grid with the questions listed vertically from the top to the bottom on the left-hand side of the chart and the names of the organizations listed left to right across the top. It will be very easy to read and to see trends.

Growth of Major Gifts in the Aggregate

The next thing to study is the major gifts given to this organization historically since its beginning or at least as far back as records go. Record in each year the dollar amount of major gifts. If your organization has not defined what a major gift is in terms of dollars, you will need to have an arbitrary threshold, such as all gifts over $5,000 in one lump sum. Then you can graph the growth or decline of these gifts.

If you have shown a growth rate in the aggregate, project that growth rate *at the same rate of increase* for the next ten years to determine the future level of major giving in projected dollar amounts.

Analysis of Prior Planned Gifts

Next, you should list all prior closed planned and deferred gifts for the past ten years (those "over the transom," including bequests) by type and dollar amounts in the aggregate (not by donor) and by the date the gift was closed. Every organization has some planned gifts, even without a program. Juxtaposed to this, list all revenue actually **received** from these gifts by type and amounts and by date received (i.e., date of death of donor to a trust or bequest distribution from an estate) for comparison and for timing. This should show you the growth rate without dedicated staff and volunteer effort in planned giving.

This should also then be reported by grid analysis, with the year across the top and the four categories down the left side: closed planned gifts (in dollars), bequest intentions, bequest revenue and trust and planned gift revenue received.

Projections

Based on all data above, **estimate** what you might receive over the next three to five years with an actively marketed program. Base this on your figures and those of the similarly situated organizations. You will be amazed to find after all of this work that a projection becomes fairly obvious. Be sure to project in each of the four categories: closed planned gifts, bequest intentions, actual planned gift revenue received and bequest revenue received. Assure the board and management that these are **estimates**, not goals!

Expenses: Preparing a Budget

First and foremost, you must figure out the budgetary process for this organization. You will need to know not only how much it will cost to achieve these projected revenues, but what the funds will be needed for. You may find that some organizations have a history of not wanting to spend on certain forms of expense. You need to know this in advance. It may well affect the ability to achieve the revenue projected above.

Budget items to consider (the actual items to be budgeted) and the amounts to be included will depend upon the "scope" of the program you have selected and how much or little you will begin all at once. Consider these items in light of a low-budget, medium-budget or high-budget operation and develop three levels of budget — one that would be wonderful to have, one that would be sufficient, but not luxurious, and the third to be bare bones, on the edge of being insufficient — that will allow you to achieve the necessary tasks. Also, consider that a start-up program will have heavier costs in early

years in certain categories than an ongoing program.
Budget items to consider include:

- Staff salaries — including your own
- Employee benefits
- Rent
- Phone
- Office overhead (indirect costs)
- Office equipment:
  - typewriter   - calculators
  - computer   - dictaphone
  - printer   - transcriber
  - modem   - fax machine
- Fixtures and furnishings
- Office supplies — paper, letterhead, labels, other
- List purchase
- Expenses for mailings — graphics, typesetting, printing, label or mailing house
- Postage
- Brochures and newsletters in bulk (customor purchased)
- Consulting / Legal / Accounting
- Continuing professional education and association for employees
- Reimbursement for volunteers
- Entertainment and meals
- Travel and lodging
- Library — books, newsletters, journals
- Software and on-line expense
- Seminars — (speakers, refreshments, room, A-V equipment, photo-copies, postage follow-up mailings, etc.)
- New program development
- Marketing research / consultants
- Advertisements

Attach specifically projected dollar amounts to the categories above that your new program must bear. If you developed revenue estimates for three years, do expenses for three years as well. Then, for each year, calculate the gain or loss on the planned gift operations.

Determining your Yield on the Board's Investment

Having done all of the above studying and preparation, you should put your report together for the board. First, your products, next, your revenue projections, then, your proposed expenses and, finally, your calendar of activities.

State your projections as to closed gift revenues held in irrevocable vehicles, plus gift revenue actually projected to be received, plus expected receipts from bequest intentions. This is the sum of your "earnings" for the same time period for which you are requesting funds. Starting with the second year (do not use the first year's numbers), determine for each year that you have made projections what the yield is — the net revenues divided by the total amount expended to achieve these revenues. This is exactly the same procedure we used in the analysis in chapter 1 with regard to the yield on the organization's categories of revenues. This is your yield in the early years; it only gets better with time and experience. Present this to your board with your business plan. They will need to have an estimate of what their investment will buy for the organization.

You will need to ask the board for a specific dollar amount for expenses for each year for a number of years to sustain this "new enterprise" until it is self-sufficient. From your projected budget, state the total dollar amount you will need, then break it into yearly amounts.

For the same time period, you have asked for a specific amount of funds. Does your "earnings" figure exceed, match or fall below that which you asked for? If it exceeds, the excess divided by the budget request is the yield to the organization over the startup period. If it does not exceed the expense, then look to the surveyed organizations. What is their yield, excess of receipts (earnings) over budget (expenses), divided by budget expenses for a given year? How long did it take them to achieve that? These should be presented to the board for consideration. You should be able to show a positive and healthy yield by the end of five years. It is this yield that will convince the board that its funds will be well spent.

Be sure to show the net to gross figures for dollars received in program fees for the organization compared to the net to gross for dollars received in the fund-raising program. Planned giving should at least be able to achieve the same return on the dollar that annual and major giving does.

Armed with this information, both you and your board can make an informed decision about the planned giving program.

Planning the Chronology for Twelve Months and Projection for Twenty-Four Months

Working out the chronology involves setting the tasks to be done on a summary basis, then on a detailed basis. It involves considering how to communicate those tasks to those in positions above the planned giving officer.

Evaluation reports of progress will be important during the first twelve months, particularly where the number of prospects and the types of tasks are used in lieu of monetary goals. It is strongly advised that monetary *goals* not be set for at least the first twelve months, if not the first twenty-four months. This does not mean you should not have revenue *projections* in your business plan.

The reason for not setting absolute monetary goals too early is because so much underlying work needs to be done that failure to meet a monetary goal within the first year can be very discouraging to all parties involved. If it seems a monetary goal is not going to be reached, the tendency is to drop the organizational and foundation-laying work in favor of beating the bushes for a couple of gifts to make the program look good. This is truly short-term thinking and crisis management.

In particular, the executive director and the board or a planned giving volunteer committee may become extremely disheartened if they set their hopes too high (with regard to dollar amount). This is why goals and evaluations should be set on a task-by-task basis.

For example, I will do these tasks this month: (1)_____, (2)_____, (3)_____, etc. I will see X number of prospects this month. I will send X number of proposal letters over six months, etc.

List of Goals and Objectives

A. Learn about the organization
  1. Its history from present to future
  2. Develop a case for planned giving
  3. Document planned gifts already received
B. Obtain a commitment from the organization
  1. Time, both yours and others
  2. Funds
     a. Number of years the board should commit to and what dollar level for expenses
     b. Expected goals in dollars
C. Prospect analysis
  1. Analysis of current records
  2. Matrix of gift history
  3. Determine core group of prospects (basic market)
  4. Expanded markets
     a. Internal to the organization
     b. External to the organization
D. Scope of program
  1. Budget
  2. Tasks
  3. Selection of vehicles
  4. Implementation of steps necessary to put vehicles in place

E.   Marketing strategy
1.   Six-step marketing plan — written
2.   Implementation of plan
F.   Staff training — development, accounting, public relations, etc.
G.   Selection of volunteer committees
H.   Establishment of external relations
I.   Setting of planned giving policies and guidelines
1.   Policies for issues that affect the board members
2.   Guidelines to help the staff make decisions
J.   Identification of, cultivation of and "problem-solving" for prospects

Each of these goals will require that a certain set of tasks be accomplished in order to achieve that goal. In planning ahead, write out those tasks you can think of. Other tasks will make themselves known during the process.

Once those tasks are defined, spread or calendar them monthly in some order of priority over the next twelve months. They will normally break into items to be done internally and items requiring external or outreach work. These are done concurrently.

Each month you will have a list of tasks to be accomplished. As a regular process of self-evaluation, examine these same tasks and record for your own files which ones you have accomplished, and for those remaining unaccomplished record the reasons why they were not accomplished. Try to note if there is a pattern of obstacles or problems preventing you from succeeding. Then, if the same ones remain unaccomplished after two to three months, meet with your supervisor to resolve why they cannot be achieved. Use these monthly memos in your employer-employee evaluation meeting. This helps uncover obstacles early in the process.

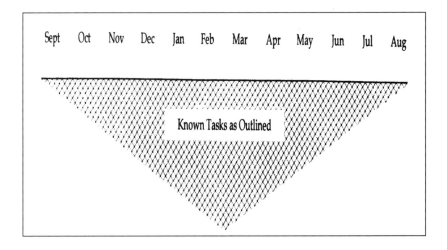

You will no doubt set too many tasks at first and they will naturally shift themselves to later dates. This spreading of tasks on a calendar is a guideline, not a right rule.

Sample Chronology

	Internal Work	External Work
Month 1	Budget Contract (understanding of employment), if not done prior Current FR effort analysis Matrix Volunteers Study of organization Meet key people	Meet with consultants, interview, select Computer systems—data Meet key people
Month 2	Board treaty Plan committees Confidentiality Ethics Committee Action Plan	Visit prospective members
Month 3	Marketing Plan Begin Planned Giving Case Traditional guidelines	Meet with selected marketing advisors Survey of trustees; interview
Month 4	Define scope of program Board Treaty approval Begin marketing brochure, funding opportunities Products	Meet with Marketing Committee Meet with Volunteer Committee Meet with Board Members Meet with Technical Advisors

	Internal Work	External Work
Month 5	Marketing Plan Internal training lunch Case Products Seminars to attend Volunteer book Begin legal work	Meet with Marketing Committee Assessment of F&A Meet with lawyers

Month 6	Core group prospects;
	  assign
	Brochures, newsletters
	Staff meetings
	Legal work
		Meet financial
		  community
		F&A procedures
		Meet with PR
		Meet with Volunteer
		  Committee

Month 7	Core group strategy
	Bequest plan
	Newsletter
	Proposals
	Legal work
	Plan donor seminars;
	  board seminars
		Meet with Marketing
		  Community
		F&A procedures

Month 8	Bequest Plan Proposals Donor seminar Board seminar Legal documents Marketing brochure	Meet with Volunteer Committee Meet with lawyer

	Internal Work	**External Work**
Month 9	Gift credit; recognition Idea mailing Target seminars Core group follow-up	Computer systems — financial Marketing Committee Board thanks (personal) to volunteers
Month 10	Staff meeting Follow-up on idea mailing Targeted seminars Follow-up	PR-media access Meet with Volunteer Committee
Month 11	Replace Committee members Recognition mailing Idea mailing Gift procedure	Meet with Technical Committee at institution Meet with Board
Month 12	Follow-up on responses Elderly program Recognition Event 12-month review	Chat cultivation Visit financial advisors Volunteer Committee

Sample Detailed Chronology
(Hypothetical)

Month 1

First, set your budget (refer to beginning of chapter) and your chronology. Then research, assess and select a consultant. Decide "on hold," "on call" or "hired."

Gather and assess information regarding all current fund-raising gifts made in a recent past term of years, either as selected by a staff member or consultant, or as the records may warrant. For example, the last three years, the last five years, the last ten years. A ten-year history is, of course, the best basis on which a good matrix may be formed. It is also a lot of work, so be prepared.

Check the computer systems available to planned giving and the capability of pulling donor data from those systems in an efficient manner. Is the program capable of a sort function based on dollar amounts, repeats and increases?

Sort by the matrix and levels (once set) as described in chapter 2. From that matrix, select a core group of prospects to work with during the first twelve months. Report these prospects, both the number of them and names of them, in the initial report to the executive branch.

Review core group prospects with the development director and/or executive for current activity and for targeted activity by other parts of the development office.

Gather names of volunteers suitable to planned giving work, but *not* on the basis of technical expertise. See chapter 5 for using certain volunteers or board members in the role of planned giving to make this assessment.

Check the organization for long-range planning studies or strategic planning studies that have been made, that have been started or that have been started and abandoned (and if so, determine for what reason).

Study the history of the organization.

The Program: Its founding, evolution, past boards and availability of board minutes.

Financial: Read at least five past annual reports and find out who managed the money and how well they performed.

Check the organization for demographic / marketing studies done in the recent past. If none, meet with the development director or executive regarding the possibility of getting such a study underway, offer explanations as to why they are necessary for planned giving.

Set up meetings of introduction between staff person and executive director, chairman of the board, chairman of the development committee, head of the finance department, public relations and others as appropriate. (Tell who you are, why you're there, what you plan to do, how it may affect their functions and vice versa. Ask who you should regularly work with, who to go to for trouble shooting.)

Month 2

Develop board policies and create a board treaty in draft form (see chapter 5). Begin to lay plans to develop three committees or three subcommittees of the development board, if one exists.

Develop the charge of each committee very clearly, in written form suitable to distribute.

Write a statement of confidentiality, review it with the development director and / or executive and prepare it for committees and staff.

Write statements on conflicts, undue influence, professionalism and fiduciary responsibility of both the planned giving staff and the board with respect to planned gifts.

Meet with executive and / or chairman of the board regarding appropriate committee members (go through six-box study regarding board members for the volunteer committee).

Select appropriate inviter for each committee member and visit each prospective volunteer committee member.

Prepare committee action time line to distribute to prospective members.

Prepare packet regarding committee membership. One packet for volunteers and one packet for the marketing committee and the technical committee. The packet should at least include a case statement of the organization, how to ask, financial statements, statement of confidentiality, initial report on matrix, hopes for marketing plan, gift vehicles and bottom-line purpose of planned giving.

Begin to set-up interviews with prospective marketing committee members and technical committee members and discuss the following:

- Who you are.
- What you plan to do.
- How you hope to accomplish it.
- Why you chose this person for help.
- Why the committee is important.
- What the time commitment is.
- How it might enhance their visibility, business.
- One exciting planned gift case.

Write material on how to evaluate the tasks in your chronology.

Interview attorneys to determine who may be hired to do the legal work for the planned giving. Be sure of the comfort level on the part of the planned giving officer with the knowledge and personality of the attorney.

Month 3

Set the marketing strategy: how to select consultant volunteers, write the plan and use matrix results (What if there is no demographic study?).

Develop a marketing plan according to the formula in chapter 4.

Based on matrix results and the marketing survey, if available, begin to develop target markets and design products for them.

Interview attorneys (continued) and CPAs (new) to work

with the planned giving program.

If no marketing survey exists and no plans will be developed to undertake one, begin constituency research to the extent possible for the organization to determine your own demographic study (see chapter 4 on marketing and communications).

Begin meeting with marketing and technical advisors on an individual basis.

Based on the history of the organization and meetings with the executive, refine the planned giving case.

Undertake a survey of trustees in your area or region who are compatible with the organization's desires to: (1) manage its own funds and use a custodian or (2) have outside trustees, interview trustees. Get fees, services, sample monthly reports and ask for references from other institutions and *check* them. Ask technical committee members' opinions. Ask the following survey questions:

- How much money under management?
- How much charitable money under management?
- How much of that in charitable trusts?
- How long and what kinds?
- Who does charitable trust accounting and tax work?
- Expertise in general counsel's office?
- How many officers with charitable trusts knowledge?
- Other charitable services?
- Fees?

Draft traditional planned giving guidelines (see chapter 8).

Month 4

Invite the marketing committee to the organization and show the members the beginnings of the marketing survey and marketing plan. Continue on the plan with their help.

Meet with the volunteer committee to go over the matrix you have formed from the results of past years' gifts. Develop the core group concept with them, show them the marketing plans that are being developed by the marketing committee and plan to submit the planned giving case to them for the next meeting.

Begin to define the scope of the program based on initial interpretation of the marketing plan, the constituency and the matrix results. Meet with the executive and director of development to confirm that you are on the right track regarding the scope of the program.

Meet with the selected lawyer to begin legal work on the gift vehicles selected, such as pooled income funds, charitable gift annuities or trusts. Get an estimate of time and fees.

Meet with outside advisors, such as real estate brokers and/ or life insurance agents, to undertake other programs within the scope.

Set meetings with key board members to discuss the progress to date, the plans for the scope of the program and the outside personnel you will use to help you get the program off the ground. Also, encourage them to sign the board treaty at this time.

Meet with the executive director regarding the same issues as above.

Meet with technical advisors separately, in their offices, to explain why you need their services and to attempt to motivate them to get involved. Ask about a seminar for advisors in the community.

Prepare funding opportunities for a marketing brochure.

Begin drafting and selecting photos for the marketing brochure.

Begin researching products available on the market:

- Library
- Software
- Donor newsletter
- Brochures

Month 5

Marketing plan continuation — meet with the marketing committee.

Meet with funds administration and begin to assess the current procedures (if any) followed for the intake of gifts and for reporting to donors.

Establish funds administration guidelines for planned gifts, vehicle-by-vehicle, and, in addition, establish review procedures in advance for various assets. Create checklists for each asset and a time frame for reviewing unusual gifts in advance of accepting the gifts, with the funds administration office.

Host a staff training seminar lunch. Make it a nice one in the nature of "here's what we are doing and how it will benefit the whole organization."

- Invite Development, PR, Funds Administration, Real Estate office and any other directly affected offices.
- Present the case you have developed, the scope of the program to be undertaken, the marketing efforts to date and the funds administration procedures that you will suggest.
- Have at least one member of each of your three committees there for goodwill and for cooperation, in addition to helping the rest of the staff see how you operate.
- Invite all important department heads, both for the administrative departments and for the direct program, such as deans for a school or doctors for a hospital.
- Include key secretaries, who will be crucial to the achievement of your goals, in this staff luncheon.

Finish the case in final form.

Finish the draft of the marketing brochure and send it around for review to necessary internal and external people.

Decide on the purchase of or drafting of brochures and newsletters, and review what is available on the market.

Continue to assess funds administration and to develop guidelines for the administration of planned gifts. Also, train key staff members.

Check upcoming seminars for personal education and update.

Continue to work on target markets and product design. Plan the first donor seminar based on the results.

Create a volunteer book which discusses the following:

- Issue orientation
- Vehicle explanation
- How to ask
- Funding opportunities available

Meet with the volunteer committee regarding core prospects, and train them on how to work with these prospects for planned gifts — perhaps use an outside consultant. Encourage board attendance at this meeting, realizing, however, that only a few members will show up. Finalize the case with the committee, present the draft of the marketing brochure up to this point and discuss funding priorities.

Continue legal work on gift vehicles and prepare documents for usage.

Month 6

Meet with key volunteers from the volunteer committee regarding the core group. Plan a volunteer committee meeting, the subject of which will be the assignment of prospects to each person. Assignments of prospects may also be made to board members not on the volunteer committee. Volunteers need to strategize, submit prospect information to the data base, research and cultivate.

Begin to hold general meetings with trust officers, attorneys, CPAs and other financial professionals in the community to let them know the following:

(1)   What you know about planned giving.
(2)   How they can help.
(3)   How they can retain their client and/or continue making money, even if a gift is made.
(4)   How they can enhance their client's position (using hypothetical cases).
(5)   Broach the subject of seminars for professionals in the community and try to stir up interest in such a concept.

Finalize meetings internally with funds administration, public relations, treasurer, real estate, etc., from month one — work out relationships.

Follow-up on selected core group cultivation meetings. Set appointments for volunteers and verify that they have made these appointments. Follow-up.

Finalize the selection of or drafting of brochures and newsletters. Set a newsletter timetable and topics.

During volunteer committee meetings: (1) go over hypothetical cases outlining certain situations where planned gifts are desirable, (2) track assignments regarding the core group and ask for reports and (3) encourage them *not* to solicit too soon.

Prepare monthly staff meeting topics for future staff meetings. For example, one good idea, gifts in, gifts structured.

Meet with the attorney regarding the legal work being done on the gift vehicles.

Prepare the six-month evaluation report.

Month 7

Continue in-office work on core group prospects, research and gift structuring to support volunteer efforts. Step-in personally where necessary. Visit, chat, maybe solicit.

Begin to draft a bequest brochure and take the first step towards an expanded market. Prepare mailing and lists.

Write or purchase a newsletter and then send it. Set a schedule.

Create proposal letter formats for each gift vehicle and put them on a word processor.

Check on the status of the legal documents for each vehicle.

Meet with the volunteer committee regarding the core group. Go over the assets, needs and objectives, contacts made or needed (if they need help), meetings that they have had, progress they have made, present the bequest brochure and mailing plans. Pretend that you are the donor.

Plan for a series of donor seminars by preparing the following:

- Target markets
- Speakers
- Materials
- Mailings
- Room, etc.

Plan a board seminar with an outside speaker.

Continue helping funds administration gear-up for administering planned gifts.

Month 8

Finish the bequest brochure and prepare a mailing.

Finalize sample proposal letters to be used on a regular basis. Circulate them for comments.

Continue plans for a donor seminar, following up with speakers and attendees (check who is coming and get board help).

Hold a board seminar. Evaluate.

Hold a donor seminar. Evaluate.

Obtain final legal documents — make sure you understand every word.

Have a general marketing brochure ready to use. Buy, or have prepared, back-up brochures or word-processed text regarding individualized situations for target markets or gift vehicles.

Work with the marketing committee to create pieces for identified target markets — determine the text, the product, the method of reaching the targeted markets and the return information method.

Hold a monthly staff meeting for thirty to forty-five minutes.

Discuss one idea or one gift made.

Meet with the volunteer committee regarding assignments, research uncovered, proposed strategy and follow-up on any visits.

Meet with the board chairman or executive regarding reaching those board members not on the core group list.

Seek speaking engagements before lawyer groups, CPAs, financial planners, etc.

Pursue special-use pooled income funds.

Realize that once you begin something during one month it never seems to end, so that each month your workday grows.

Realize that you and the committees are entering the "demoralized period," where you realize that there is still a lot of underlying work to do, perhaps no gifts have come in up to this point and perhaps you have received rejections from all of your core group.

Realize you are nearing the end of the preparatory stage and that you really need to start cultivating, and then soliciting. The next era is that of trying to get donors in the door.

1 to 6-12 months	12 to 24-36 months	36 months on
Prep	Struggle to get donors, cultivation mostly	Gift Flow, Gift Administration

Check back with funds administration. Also check to see that all systems are set to go and that the computer systems are in place.

Report informally to the board, committees and executive on tasks originally set, those accomplished and those outstanding. (This is a follow-up to the six-month written evaluation.)

Meet with the volunteer committee regarding the core group, the bequest program and any turn-ups from seminars or staff.

- Research and assign
- Meet with prospect (suspect)
- Follow-up with proposal (written to donor/attorney)

Month 9

Ask certain board members, not on committees, to help motivate volunteers/solicitors by taking them (personally) to lunch or a social event, etc., where they say, "Thanks, we understand all the good work you are doing. Keep up the good work."

Develop gift credit guidelines.

Develop recognition vehicles, such as the following:

- Clubs
- Dinners
- Premiums, etc.

Send a mailing of one (and only one) interesting idea to local financial advisors. Call key people on the technical advisory committee and ask them to make phone calls to the key community lawyers, CPAs, etc., about the mailing — check and follow-up.

Meet with the marketing committee to go over the development of plans so far and ask advice on ads, newspaper coverage (include PR in the discussions) and releases to be coordinated with organizational PR work.

Prepare a series of seminars to go on for at least the next twelve months covering the following:

(1) Target groups, such as donors, regarding separate subjects.
(2) Advisors and how they can retain clients and make money in this market.
(3) Specific topics, such as planning for real estate, estate planning for singles, tax planning for year-end, etc.
(4) Marketing strategy for all development officers to help them leverage your efforts.

Further work with the core group to identify any expanded markets which may have started. Work with the marketing committee to identify new groups, and how to approach and follow-up with the volunteer group regarding assignments and what research they may need.

Newsletter article.

Hold a monthly staff meeting.

Month 10

Use the monthly staff meeting for the planned gifts / major gifts staff to indicate the stage of proposals sent out and prospects uncovered, and the cultivation techniques used. Also, indicate that chat is important, and explain how to help older people, staying within fixed guidelines.

Follow-up donor meetings with letters, proposals and newly discovered strategies (taken from update newsletters, journals, etc.). Recognize the importance of continual contact.

Do the same type of "new strategies" letter to all committees and the board, and make phone call follow-ups to *all those people* regarding the new strategy to turn up potential leads.

Work with the PR department to gain media access and visibility.

Start targeted seminars for small groups of eight to fifteen people and follow-up individually.

Month 11

Invite the technical advisory committee to lunch at the institution. Discuss the program and its progress, and try to get the members to volunteer for non-charitable giving positions at the organization.

Invite the marketing group to lunch at the institution, do the same as above.

Replace committee members (by this time you have probably had a turn over of one-third to one-half of your committee members and you will need to work on restructuring the committees).

Meet with the board chairman and/or executive to follow-up on both board and volunteer committee solicitations, to try to close gifts with some core group prospects, to present interesting structures and to publicize if possible.

Conduct a mailing — new strategy, "one good idea," — to all affiliated advisors, and follow-up with the technical committee who will follow-up with their colleagues with phone calls.

Conduct a mailing, to the core group and to any responders in the new expanded markets, regarding newly created gift clubs and what a donor's dollars can buy (funding opportunities).

Read, read, read to find new ideas.

Work with funds administration or the bank on any closed gifts and iron out the new procedures.

Employee evaluation by supervisor, use task self-evaluation memos and ask for a raise if you have been successful in accomplishing tasks, or seek modification to contract if necessary.

Hold a monthly staff meeting.

Month 12

Follow-up on any inquiries that have come in, and follow-up on all meetings with letters, gift proposals and gift structures.

Have chat sessions with anyone whose name you now have, activate your listening strategy, make copious file notes and begin true long-term cultivation for those attenuated prospects (suspects).

Visit selected financial professionals to report your progress and ask about their clients, *but only* with regard to one or two pre-selected strategies or target markets. Do not use a shotgun approach.

Meet with the volunteer committee and review the past twelve months.

Develop a "help the elderly donor" strategy and put yourself out a little bit for personal help, but review ethics guidelines.

Hold a recognition event for all three committees and for key board members and staff members who have been important to the program.

Report progress by task. Also, report any gifts and any actual earnings.

Hold a monthly staff meeting.

Prepare the twelve-month evaluation report.

Months 12-24 — The Hard Months: A Projection

- Clubs.
- Advisors.
- Seminars and newsletters.
- Another board presentation.
- Much chat with year one suspects.
- Begin to chat with year two suspects.
- Meet with committees quarterly.
- Self-educate and seminars for update.
- PR/Media.
- Monitor funds administration procedures, tax returns.
- Watch legislation and tax reform.
- Educate development staff and funds administration board if there are major changes and use the opportunity for a message.
- TAKE TWO FULL WEEKS OF VACATION AT ONE TIME WITHOUT FAIL. FORGET THE OFFICE AND THE PRESSURE TO RAISE MONEY.
- Make timid to strong attempt, depending on the first year, to set monetary goals with some disclaimers, particularly if it is a brand new program.
- Attend update seminars and/or industry seminars to keep in contact with colleagues.
- Learn other facets of fund raising from staff members in your office who are involved in phone-a-thons, special

events, corporations and foundations. Leads may turn up here.

- Check business ventures. Can you joint venture with some of your entrepreneurial types?
- Conduct many, many personal visits and chats. Strengthen your listening strategies, strengthen your file notes and use your computer database entries.
- Get active in a planned giving roundtable if you have not already done so. Give volunteer time, be an officer, meet people.

Evaluations: Of Self and Program, by Supervisors

Evaluation should track tasks as set in the chronology.

Six-month evaluations should be in memo form outlining the following: (1) tasks set to undertake, (2) tasks actually undertaken, (3) success, failure and incompleteness, (4) why (for number three) and (5) what help you need (specifically) to accomplish incomplete or failed tasks.

Address the memo to your immediate supervisor with copies to the executive and to the chairman of the board. Provide a line for initials and a space for comments by each. Follow-up to see that you get it back filled out or just initialed.

Consider more frequent, private self-evaluations. Monthly evaluations should be in the same form, but they should only go to your immediate supervisor. Meet with him/her every month to go over the report. Get it initialed.

Month 1

Reached employment understanding; developed budget and got approval; developed matrix and identified a specific number of prospects.

Month 2

Achieved the first draft of the Board Treaty; proposed three committees, met with prospective committee members.

Month 3

Developed a draft of the marketing plan and circulated it; drafted a case and circulated it; drafted guidelines and circulated them.

Month 4

Set the scope of program after the guidelines were circulated; held meetings with all three committees and the board members.

Month 5

Developed the marketing plan with the marketing committee; hosted a staff lunch; circulated a volunteer book; and selected and approved a law firm.

Month 6 and Half-Year

X number of core prospects researched and assigned to volunteers; administrative procedures begun; selections made for mailers (attached); reviewed first six months in a report and circulated it to the executive, the development director, the chairman of the board and, perhaps, key board members — indicated to what degree you were lagging according to the timeline.

Month 7

Created the core group prospect report — number seen, number called, number of proposals sent out; set expanded market plan by doing (list what was done).

Month 8

Continued core group visits and proposals (describe); created a report on seminars — number attended, questions asked, proposed follow-up, how many leads (potential) generated ("turnips").

Month 9

Created plans for clubs, etc.; created one idea letter; core group visits and number of those seen, etc.

Month 10

Sent idea mailing; reviewed results of seminars, follow-ups, potential leads; and attached any media coverage to the report.

Month 11

Included copies of mailings; reported follow-ups regarding leads; and reported new committee members.

Month 12 and Year

Report on cultivation meetings, elderly outreach and the recognition event; 12-month recap — Where is the program lagging? Why? Where might you need help? Report on (1) the total prospects seen, (2) the total number of written proposals sent out, (3) the total number of signed gifts and (4) the actual dollars received.

This evaluation process, conducted on a regular basis, will serve three purposes. First, you will see what you have accomplished. Second, you will discover where the recurring obstacles are and can work with those around you to overcome them. And third, your supervisor will get a good picture of how the program is developing and where s/he may need to step-in to help or back you up.

Report

	Contacts Made	Prospects Seen	Written Proposal	Gifts in Process	Closed Gift	Revenue Rec'd
Month 6						
Month 12						
Month 18						
Month 24						
Month 30						
Month 36						

This is the bare minimum report that should be kept on an ongoing basis for your evaluations and reports. It would be better if you keep your inputs more thoroughly and on data base software.

4

The Marketing Plan

It takes all the running you can do to keep in the same place. If you want to get somewhere else, you must run at least twice as fast as that!
— Said the Queen in *Alice in Wonderland*
by Lewis Carroll

O nce you have your business plan in place, you will want to activate your fund-raising efforts. Part of your business plan was the analysis of the market outreach of other, similar organizations. As a coordinated effort, you must have a written marketing plan in conjunction with (and to carry out) your business plan.

What is "marketing" other than a buzzword? In the early 1980s, the idea of marketing became an important element in conversations concerning planned giving success. It seemed that if you didn't use the word, you really weren't "in." While plenty of people did use the word, not too many used the concept.

Planned giving consultants and seminar presenters are among those who have helped the word flourish, but have they fulfilled the promise of delivering marketing to the planned giving population?

We tend to think of marketing in terms of mailings, brochures and seminars. These vehicles of communication, however, are just that; communication. Marketing is something wholly different. New, fresh thinking must occur. Breakthroughs, such as spending at least as much of your budget for marketing consultants or staff members as for lawyers or technically-oriented planned giving staff, would be a large step in the right direction.

Many practictioners in the field focus on gift vehicles and taxes because tax technicalities may cause them fears and insecurities. They often turn away opportunities to learn marketing and management principles as they relate to planned giving and opt, instead, for courses in gift design or taxes. However, to use the technical information learned in those courses **you must have a prospect to talk to**. Finding those prospects and then getting them to meet with you one-on-one is your goal. Without effective marketing you may as well "talk tax technical" to the closest wall. You will waste time, knowledge and money by attending tax-oriented seminars without learning how to acquire fruitful markets that you can address with your message

Let's look beyond the buzzword. Statistics show that there are fifteen million businesses in this country, about ninety-seven percent of which are classified as small businesses. Only one in five start-up businesses still exist after four to five years. Do most of these businesses eventually fail because their product or service is not good? Probably not. It is more likely that marketing and management has been inadequate. They either failed to promote their product or service appropriately, or they failed to manage their operation efficiently. Planned giving is exactly like a small business in this case.

It might help to better define marketing for our purposes. In "A Conceptual Approach to Marketing," an essay published by the American Marketing Association, William McInnes begins by identifying a market. He says simply, "The gap between the producer and the consumer is the market." In essence, markets result from the exchange of goods and services, where people are seeking to satisfy their wants and needs through that exchange.

Others have also started here. E.T. Grether explains that a market is business activities involved in directing the flow of goods and services from the producer to the consumer or user, which centers around multiple geographic markets. The behavior of the firm adjusts its horizontal spatial relationships to industrial, regional and national groups.

John R. Commons says a market is something institutional rather than geographical. He says it is patterns of collective action in control of individual action which makes markets (hence the theory, center on institutions rather than on individual actions). Marketing is primarily a physical function made necessary because of the separation of production and consumption.

Yet another stream of thought treats marketing as a process actuated by the interplay of actions between various individuals cooperating under the division of labor, the basic concept being one of equilibrium of supply and demand.

Edmund D. McGarry relates to the classifications of those activities which constitute the *sine qua non* of marketing. In other words, how many tasks make up marketing. This is considered a functional approach.

Marketing theory can be very challenging and can make your head spin. However, there are some easy concepts and principles that will help move your program along that you should learn, if you do not already know them.

Before going any further, let's break this concept down into three aspects of marketing.

Market — Echoing McInnes' view, the market is that space or gap that separates consumers and producers; the consumer-producer relationship necessarily exists, but at a distance. The producer must survey the territory to determine who out there needs the product. The gap between the producer and consumer still exists.

Market Relation Between Producer and Consumer — A *foundation* exists for an exchange, but is not a substitute for it; the market is real, but it is not yet realized. While the market relationship may be in existence, it is still a potential exchange. A prospect is identified, but is not yet a consumer.

Marketing is the *catalyst that closes the gap*, the process of realization or actualization. It is the totality of the activity that makes the producer and consumer connect.

Now let's look at a chart depicting these concepts:

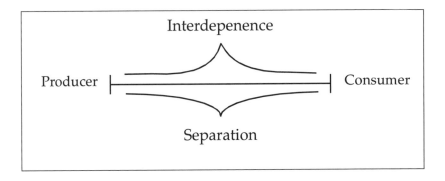

In the fund-raising world, we do not ordinarily think in terms of producers and consumers. Nevertheless, organizations serve in the role of the producer of gift opportunities and the donor is the consumer of those opportunities. We need to think along these lines.

There is a real separation between producers and consumers when you realize that the maker of the goods does not necessarily use the goods, and that the provider of the service does not necessarily benefit from the service. Despite the separation, they are necessarily related because this separation is accompanied by an interdependence; as soon as a person produces a good or service, s/he is in the market for a consumer. As soon as a person develops the capacity to consume, s/he is in the market for a producer. That is what the market is, this real, interdependent relationship between producer and consumer.

The force, or catalyst, making a potential market contact into a real market contact is generally what is known as marketing. Marketing is any "motion" or activity that actualizes the potential relation of the producer and consumer. Marketing in its widest sense, therefore, is any activity which actualizes the potential market relationship between the makers and users of economic goods and services.

There are dimensions of the market potential, however. It is only when the *dimensions of the market* are determined that the corresponding dimensions of the *marketing task* can be determined.

Market task and market potential are inseparably linked; marketing makes the contact that ends separation and it bridges the gap between producer and consumer. What are the dimensions of the market?

Space **separation** of parties. Parties must get together in some way for an exchange to occur. Whether this means in person or by some other means, the gap must be closed.

Separation in *time.* There is necessarily a time lag between production and consumption. Every market situation includes a time factor.

Perceptional **separation.** Consumers do not know what is available and producers do not know where the consumers are. There is always a separation of information and persuasion. The fewer consumers who know about or are interested in the product, the greater the market potential. When customers are well informed and highly motivated, the remaining market potential is smaller.

Separation of *ownership.* No exchange is completed until title of ownership is transferred.

Separation of *values.* The producer measures his/her sacrifice in terms of costs and competition and, therefore, sets an offering price. The consumer measures his/her satisfaction in terms of usefulness in his/her situation and the ability to pay.

If a market represents a separation — in space, time, perception, value and ownership — between producer and consumers, then some force is required to bridge the gap and bring them together. That force, or activity, is what we call *marketing.*

Each of the five dimensions discussed above — space, time, perception, ownership and value — can keep donor and donee apart. Marketing is the creative force acting upon these five potential gaps to get donor and donee moving forward together. Let us look at each of these five with respect to planned giving:

(1)   **Space.** Space actualization involves designing a charitable arrangement for target-markets, delivery of the message via various forms of media, particularizing for an individual prospective donor and then meeting, de-

(2)   **Time.** Marketing motions place the goods a customer wants before him/her at the moment s/he wants them. Deliver information before a donor chooses a non-charitable option.

(3)   **Ownership.** Taking ownership embraces all the motions of transferring the title from the producer to the consumer. Asset transfer planning and implementation must be made easy for donors.

(4)   **Value.** Aligning the seller's bids and the buyer's offers (price policy). This involves getting the donor to commit assets to obtain triple-dipping tax benefits; it also includes donor selection of charity and options for restricted or general use.

(5)   **Perception.** Your communication brings within the perception of consumers the gift plans that are available. What is perceived is more real than "real." It is manifested in the activities of disseminating information and of persuasion, the former to overcome the lack of knowledge of the potential, the latter to overcome the inertia and get the donor to do something. Perceptional actualization involves converting the "consumer" into a "donor;" acceptance of irrevocable transfer; understanding of the areas of flexibility and/or rigidity of the gift vehicles.

The end result is a market transaction and the satisfaction of consumer wants.

The concept of marketing may, at first glance, frighten a practical business person. It would not, however, be as frightening if the concept were translated into the concrete phrase: if you wish to be successful as a marketing agent, you must first determine when, where, who and at what price consumers want your product, and then you must arrange to tell people about your product, motivate them to buy it and get it to the right people when, where and in the way they want it.

It is not marketing research information, but *action* based on correct information that can yield results.

Let us delve further into perception and how it adjusts the consumer to the product. First, how do perceptions and images get formed? Facts are obviously the starting point, but just the facts are not sufficient. Perception must be molded around the facts. Perception is something that is created inside the mind of the prospect and was no doubt created long ago.

A part of marketing is to mold perception around the facts. It is the *creation* of the perception of the facts. You have an opportunity to *create* perception when the concept is new. Media is one vehicle of communication to deliver the molded facts to the inside of the prospect's mind.

Creating perceptions is easier than changing them. Think about it. Think about Kleenex, a company that has become synonymous with its product, tissue. The same can be said for Xerox. The perception has been created that these companies *are* their products.

New Coke, however, is an example of a failed effort to change perceptions. Changing perceptions is always harder than creating new ones. Marketing and facts must work together so that the name is attached to its perceptional value. Above all, marketing approaches must always be positive, upbeat and exciting.

Can perception creation be used in planned giving? Yes, we can mold the facts to fit comfortably inside the mind of the prospective donor, but we must take the mind as we find it. We must work with the ideas and values the prospective donor already holds.

Now, what is it we want to mold? That's right, facts. Facts about the gift, the organization and the tax consequences. How do we select the mold? We use perception, needs and wants. How can we meet what the donor wants? How do we actualize it? We must communicate. Remember, information must blend with persuasion and be effectively delivered.

Before moving forward, however, let us ponder one question. Is this marketing strategy, and the planned giving market it is related to, understood and accepted by those in the field? Philip Kotler, marketing professor at Northwestern University, prepared a survey of three hundred educational administrators asking each of them, "What is marketing?"

Sixty-one percent responded that marketing is selling, advertising and public relations, twenty-eight percent of them said that it is one of those three and a very small percent said that it is needs assessment, market research, product development, pricing and distribution. In general, the nonprofit market, and the development market in particular, is not fully aware of the true nature of marketing. The planned giving field seems too preoccupied with vehicles and multi-page computer printouts when it could and should be focusing on more basic things, especially at the beginning stages.

If we look at the history of marketing in for-profit organizations over the past century, we will find three phases of activity: product orientation, consumer orientation and, what we will call, perception engineering (or, the battle for the mind).

Product orientation was a phase that focused on the product, touting it as the "best" or the most "new and improved." Long before the Pillsbury Dough Boy rolled (pun intended) into town, flour was among the many products marketed in this rather straightforward and somewhat boring manner. "Buy Pillsbury Flour. It is the best flour." Focus was on the product.

An improved economy in the late 1950s and growth in competition forced a shift toward consumer orientation. Rather than continuing to hail the product, manufacturers began focusing on the needs and wants of the consumer, targeting the June and Ward Cleaver generation.

Instant flour, for example, was developed and pitched as a quick and essential ingredient in America's meat and potatoes diet. In this instance, not only did the marketing strategy change, but the product itself changed and was fashioned to meet the needs and wants of the consumer. No lumpy gravy for the Cleavers.

Of course, this approach continued through the 1980s and 1990s and has recently evolved into another phase, the battle for the mind. Perception engineering is the act of making people believe they want or need something they had yet to consider. Today you are more likely to see an ad campaign that not only tells you that the flour you need is unbleached, but that it also has bran and is healthy.

Jeep is another great example of perception engineering. In the face of studies that showed no need or want for four-wheel drive cars or trucks in the automotive marketplace, Jeep introduced a sports utility vehicle designed for the rugged outdoor type who likes to ride in luxury. Not only did they blend two exciting concepts, they created a perception of the kind of man or woman who would be adventurous yet sophisticated enough to get behind the wheel. One look at the roads today and the results are obvious. Almost every auto manufacturer now has something similar on the market, and Mercedes and BMW are getting into the act as well.

Before looking at how all of this relates to the nonprofit arena, let us consider a few problems in this seemingly unending battle for the mind.

In the book *Positioning*, by Ries and Trout and published by Warner Books, the authors wonder what happens when everyone is customer or consumer oriented. If this tactic no longer achieves marketing results, the competition starts to get brutal and there is an inundation in the market place.

How do we get our one little message across when the mind does not want to receive any more information? According to the authors, we need to *focus on the receiving side,* not on the sending side, and over-simplify the message.

Remember, first impressions are lasting impressions. In the era of inundation of information, we need to cut through all the information that does not compute and get ranked higher and higher in the mind of the prospect. We need to do this by playing by the rules.

The book's cardinal rule is "What's in a name?" The first impression or the door opener is the most important. The difference in the way you tell it can mean everything and, as you might have guessed, the planned giving community is not yet up to speed on this, the battle for the mind phase.

Compare the following planned giving pitches: "How to support your children's purchase of a business with the help of a charitable remainder net-income unitrust with deficiency make-up clause," versus "Give your kids the business." Or compare "Depreciation pass-thru pooled income fund to build a building," with "Build us up!" The differences between these examples demonstrates the difference in molding perceptions to the mind.

Now consider these meaningless names — Telesis, Allegis, Unisys. They sure seem like lazy names as opposed to Die Hard battery. Compare in our field the pooled income fund with gift annuity. The latter name says it all. Also think about the wealth replacement trust.

Whether a name is good or bad is not necessarily relevant. The key is whether the name is appropriate and gets inside of the mind of the prospect. Baseball, hot dogs, apple pie and Chevrolet is certainly a say-nothing yet say-everything phrase. Again, you never get a second chance to make a first impression. Drop the planned giving jargon and use language non-professionals can understand.

Marketing, even for planned giving, is definitely entering a new era. Competition is brutal and the game has become about taking business away from someone else as much as it is about gaining business. Plain old aggressiveness and doggedness is not always the sign of the winner. Simply redoubling one's efforts just won't do; one must re-create and get smart. Marketing battles are not won in the customer's office or in the aisle of the grocery store, not in Detroit or Tokyo, but inside the mind of the prospect. Remember, you must take the mind as you find it. You must relate to what is already there.

Using these ideas in planned giving is unique, in that every organization operates in a segmented market and markets. Each organization must effectively communicate with each market based on its ideas, its goals and its needs.

In order to do so, an organization must analyze who it is in relation to the public as a whole, and figure out what segment or segments of society it does draw from or could draw from.

To draw from those identified segments, the organization must have something specific to offer as an exchange. An obvious example is a community college, which offers educational opportunities to various members of the community.

Once the market segment is identified then, with respect to planned giving, the organization must realistically assess that market to determine how to reach it with its information.

Peter Drucker says, "Marketing should make selling super-fluous." In planned giving, marketing should make a hard ask or a "sale" superfluous. Marketing for planned giving should create the demand that makes the undertaking of transfer into a gift ve-hicle a logical thing to do. You simply solve a problem for the do-nor or family.

Let us break this down into a simple definition. Planned giv-ing marketing is the process of identifying target markets, assess-ing and identifying the wants and needs of those markets, creating perceptions of meeting those wants and needs with planned gift vehicles, effectively communicating that perception to the prospects and effectively implementing the gift transaction.

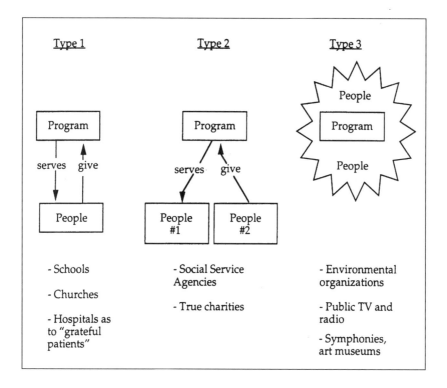

Identifying the planned giving market is better understood when looking at the three marketing models, which are outlined in the chart above. They are listed by type and distinguished by their relationship to their constituents and/or their market. The chart identifies and demonstrates who they serve and who they target for funding.

Type 1 is the closed marketing system — organizations serving a particular group that also rely on that group for some degree of funding. Type 1 organizations need less educational and visibility-type communications with the market because their constituency is their market. Their constituency is already familiar with, and invested in, their services, which means they can move more quickly toward the benefits of planned giving vehicles. These types of organizations include churches, schools and hospitals.

Type 2 are organizations of the open marketing system, where they serve one group, but look to others for financial investment. Social service agencies and charities fall under this type. With these organizations, plenty of education, visibility and selling of the "intangible product" must occur before presentations regarding planned giving vehicles can be made. The organization must communicate who it is, what need it serves, why that need is important, why this organization does it better than others delivering the same service and why someone should fund it. Then, the financial benefits of planned giving vehicles can come into play. However, if the initial step is missed, it is not likely that a gift will be made.

Organizations in **Type 3** of the marketing model are a bit of a hybrid, in that the program's product or service is an intangible benefit that people "sort of" enjoy or experience, but are not closely and directly related to in the way of a religious or educational affiliation. Like an environmental agency, the service generally improves the quality of life around the person and the person must appreciate and understand that benefit. The intangible benefit deriving from the program's existence, and benefiting those people it touches, must be firmly communicated in order to tighten up the linkage, which then leads to the ability to communicate planned giving vehicles.

The depth and the level of marketing activity will greatly differ among these three types of organizations. In fact, the choice of communication methods — such as mailings of brochures and newsletters, presentation of seminars and personal contact — will be affected by the type of organization. For example, a Type 2 organization will need to have a more savvy, professionally-designed marketing piece that catches the eye in order to inform in the quickest way possible. This is generally used prior to planned giving mailings and will reinforce what program is actually offered and to whom. The givers need to know why they like the service offered.

A person in marketing will also help determine to what extent such things as newspaper, radio or television advertising is necessary. For example, you rarely find Type 1 organizations employing modes of direct advertising in the media to solicit gifts. However, Type 2 organizations heavily use such methods of communication because they are not as close to their constituents and must reach them by these avenues. Type 3 organizations are somewhere in between, as usual, and they use these media methods of communication to some degree, but not as commercially as Type 2 organizations. Quite often the communication is more "community-benefit" or "public service" oriented.

Having reviewed some basic concepts about markets and marketing, it is time to push on. In launching a planned giving program, it is essential to develop a marketing plan. Again we recall the wisdom of Yogi Berra, "If you don't know where you're going, it may be difficult to get there." There are six basic steps to follow:

Step One: Find out who your market is.
Step Two: Segment the market into target markets.
Step Three: Design "products" to meet needs discovered in each segment, or target market.
Step Four: Research the competition, and find your "unique position."
Step Five: Create channels of communication to reach each segment uncovered in the outreach.
Step Six: Package the vehicle for the individual prospect.

Before outlining and examining these steps, however, it is

time to confront some hard truths. Is your organization ready and able to take on the market research task? Are you capable of analyzing and maintaining gift history and donor records?

Are you ready to take Step One and find out who your market is? Start with general research to determine the broadest base that might actually give to your organization in the form of a planned gift vehicle.

Then conduct or hire a market/donor survey in order to create donor profiles. Search for demographic information, such as sex, age, marital status, level of education, residence and size of family. Also gather psychographic information and data on interest in the nonprofit market (sitting on boards or volunteering for organizations, religious affiliation, civic activities, specific interests in the organization doing the survey).

Other information should be of a more financial and career oriented nature, such as one's occupation, type of organization where one is employed, income range, need for or participation in retirement planning, estate planning information, wills and trusts, ownership of small businesses, etc. Be advised that the design of a market survey is an art form and should be done with the help of a professional marketing research consultant.

Develop a matrix that includes the following: how many years recorded, totals for each segment of the office recorded and individual gifts within each segment recorded. Do you have the ability to categorize, sort and summarize?

Can you look at and consistently track each segment? Can you measure an overall increase due to donor acquisition or an increase in repeat donor's gift size? Is the incidence of repeat gifts traceable per donor? Can you measure the increase in gifts per donor? Can you measure the gaps in giving?

The resulting matrix may show that planned giving is not yet achievable. Marketing studies, product design, education, visibility and long-term cultivation may be necessary first. The results will indicate how long it will be before a planned giving program can be assimilated. These concepts will be explored in greater detai in a forthcoming book to be publishing by Precept Press.

I. Gift History
  A. Total gift amounts by whatever categories are already established (annual, major, planned, etc.) for 3, 5 or 10-year history
  B. Gifts by dollar level
    1. All gifts over $100 for the past 3, 5 or 10 years
    2. All gifts over $500 for the past 3, 5 or 10 years (broken out from number 1 above)
    3. All gifts over $1,000 for the past 3, 5 or 10 years (broken out from number 2 above)
    4. All gifts over $5,000 for the past 3, 5 or 10 years (broken out from number 3 above)
    5. All gifts over $10,000 for the past 3, 5 or 20 years (broken out from number 4 above)
    6. All gifts over $25,000 for the past 3, 5 or 20 years (broken out from number 5 above)
II. Gift Analysis
  A. Increase in giving by *category*
    1. Compare the number of gifts between $500 and $1,000 in each of the years of history
    2. Compare the number of gifts between $1,000 and $5,000 in each of the years of history
    3. Compare the number of gifts between $5,000 and $10,000 in each of the years of history
    4. Compare the number of gifts between $10,000 and $25,000 in each of the years of history
    5. Compare the number of gifts of $25,000 and up for each of the years of history
  B. Incidence of giving by *individual* donors
    1. Gifts of $500 to $1,000
      a. *Who*, by name, among those donors were repeat givers
      b. *How many*, totally, were repeat givers
    2. Gifts of $1,000 to $5,000
      a. *Who*, by name, among those donors were repeat givers
      b. *How many*, totally, were repeat givers

3. Gifts of $5,000 to $10,000
   a. *Who*, by name, among those donors were repeat givers
   b. *How many*, totally, were repeat givers
4. Gifts of $10,000 to $25,000
   a. *Who*, by name, among those donors were repeat givers
   b. *How many*, totally, were repeat givers
5. Gifts of $25,000
   a. *Who*, by name, among those donors were repeat givers
   b. *How many*, totally, were repeat givers

C. Increase in gift level by *repeat* donors
1. Gifts of $500 to $1,000
   a. Who moved into the next higher level over the years of history
   b. Did that increased level hold steady or increase more
2. Gifts of $1,000 to $5,000
   a. Who moved into the next higher level over the years of history
   b. Did that increased level hold steady or increase more
3. Gifts of $5,000 to $10,000
   a. Who moved into the next higher level over the years of history
   b. Did that increased level hold steady or increase more
4. Gifts of $10,000 to $25,000
   a. Who moved into the next higher level over the years of history
   b. Did that increased level hold steady or increase more
5. Gifts of $25,000
   a. Who moved into the next higher level over the years of history
   b. Did that increased level hold steady or increase more

III. Identify the core group
IV. Compare names to the board and committee lists

This core group of donors is the first of your marketing pools. Non-donors who are already affiliated with the organization make up your second pool. Your community at large — whether geographic or by commonality of interest — is your third pool of prospects, who may be reached directly or indirectly through financial professionals. Each of these three pools of prospects has target markets.

Prospect Pool From Your Donor Base

XYZ Medical Center Foundation
Gift Summary History by Giving Category
Number of Donors

Dollar Range	1992	1991	1990	1989	1988
$0-49	5,505	4,751	5,245	6,759	8,508
50-99	1,971	1,757	1,819	1,889	1,896
100-249	1,794	1,811	1,816	1,784	1,492
250-499	555	492	510	443	392
500-999	302	299	298	279	277
1000-4999	429	449	347	286	313
5000-9999	79	93	49	45	42
10,000-24,999	55	52	49	41	36
25,000-49,999	25	15	12	8	14
50,000-over	21	14	8	10	11
TOTAL	10,736	9,733	10,155	11,544	12,981

In this example, you have two distinct breaks and three distinct groups of donors. A natural break occurs at $250 and again at $5,000. Depending on staff time, do the gift history analysis and review individual records at either break for likely planned gift prospects. This is only pool one out of three pools.

After gaining this information, Step Two involves further market segmentation along different lines, where we begin to determine where these groups fall out with similar characteristics. In Step One we found three pools — donors, non-donor affiliates and non-donor general community. In planned giving, we have some natural, built-in markets, such as retirees, those planning for retirement, people with large homes looking to sell down, those looking to enter retirement communities, etc. It is our job to find those potential donors.

In the November 1985 issue of *Trusts and Estates*, Gregory W. Osko wrote "Divide and Conquer, One Bank's Marketing Story." The bank's markets discussed in this article are very similar to a nonprofit planned giving program's markets. Mr. Osko proposed a two-step method for market segmentation. First, determine the current market segments and identify them as recipients of targeted information, and second, determine the primary characteristics and needs of each of those markets. For example, the following list was created for the bank:

(1)   Beneficiaries
(2)   Retirees and widows
(3)   Business owners
(4)   Professionals
(5)   The middle market
(6)   Professionally managed businesses
(7)   Not-for-profit institutions

From this list Mr. Osko then took one of the segmented markets, retirees and widows, and identified the fundamental characteristics and needs of that group, as follows:

(1)   Preservation of their capital
(2)   Generating a safe, stable, sufficient and growing income on which to live
(3)   A financial plan that continues to work when they die
(4)   A financial plan that covers disability
(5)   Minimization of income and transfer taxes
(6)   Liquidity

This strategy of segmenting markets is perfectly applicable to the planned giving market. Every time you find a group, think about what their "needs" and "wants" might be, think about their hopes and dreams. It is essential to find and/or develop the segments of your market — hopefully after a market survey has been conducted by outside professionals. But even if you do not have the funds to undertake an outside professional marketing survey, the following items may be considered target markets for planned giving in general:

(1) Stage in life (creation of wealth, preservation of wealth, retirement or disposition of wealth)

(2) Need to support others, such as elderly or physically or mentally disabled relatives

(3) Need for shelter from taxes

(4) Need to dispose of property (and possibly reluctance to do so due to capital gains)

(5) No more need for a large house

(6) No use for a vacation home

(7) Collectors — desire to dispose of collections of assets, such as art, antiques and the like, or to have them preserved

(8) Business owners — transfer of assets to retirement plan or transfer to next generation

(9) Need to educate self or others (children, grandchildren)

(10) Retirees — the need to preserve capital

(11) Widows — the need for money management and capital preservation

(12) Professionals — the need to prepare for retirement while earning income

(13) Women — a different approach to philanthropy

(14) Singles (no marital deduction)

(15) Planning for and during retirement

(16) Past employees — rewarding past service and loyalty

For each of the above listed potential target markets, some of which are narrow and some of which are broad, a listing of concerns should be made.

Step Three of developing a marketing plan involves designing products to meet the needs discovered in the previous step. We are developing a marketing strategy for each target group.

If a couple is looking to buy down, think of ways you can help. How about helping them form a charitable remainder trust? Maybe they are planning for retirement, what are the possibilities of starting a deferred gift annuity or net-income unitrust? How about interesting grandparents in an education unitrust or using the pooled income fund as a product to meet various other needs? Maybe someone would like to honor a loved one with a memorial. Perhaps there is a potential for a you-can-take-it-with-you wealth replacement trust. Get to know your market, get to know the individuals and their situation and consider ways you can help them while they help you and your organization. You have to be the idea person.

Then, Step Four, research your competition. Research the type of competition you have with the same type of organization or services that you provide. Why? You want to position yourself to find out what the persuasive element is.

Find out what is offered by others, to whom, why and how successful? Discover what is unique, special and different about your organization. How do you compare? Do your presentation materials represent your uniqueness?

Research your market competition based on the level of your organization and the community it addresses — local, regional or national. Why is your college better than the other? Why is your ballet troupe different than another group? What separates your hospital from another? Why would someone want to offer your organization a planned gift? You hold the answers. Your research will help you discover the secret ingredient that makes your presentation compelling to a specific market.

How are you going to reach these markets? That is Step Five, creating channels of communication and reaching out to the public.

Many organizations jump to this step at the very beginning, often with dismal results. But having undertaken all of the research above and the steps in planning, you should be able to develop effective seminars for target markets and personal mailings to target markets, and you should understand the nature of the "shotgun" approach of the newsletter to tie these all together into your broadest base.

You should also be able to place yourself within the three types of marketing models (most organizations are primarily one type with features of the other two types) and determine whether you need to go beyond seminars, brochures, newsletters, particular mailings and private contact. Again, go through each market and determine what the best channel of communication would be for each particular market — form and contact.

Your organization may require the use of public TV and radio, commercial TV and radio, newspaper ads, ads in journals and magazines and other forms of public outreach. If so, you need to determine what message you want to get across — is it who you are and what you do, or the methods of giving to you? This will be determined based upon the length of your history and the amount of effort you have spent marketing your visibility and the nature of your services, in the past.

However, keep in mind that it can never hurt to repeat what it is that you do. A description of what it is that you do must be designed from the "perception engineering" point of view, not a "product orientation" point of view.

In Step Six, you go further and package the vehicle for the individual prospect identified — one-on-one. Choose the vehicle based on the needs of the market segment in which the donor "resides." Do not inundate him / her with every possible vehicle and its explanation.

This is in the nature of "private marketing," no cookie-cutter approach permitted here. Once the product is designed for target markets, further tailoring must be undertaken for the individual in light of that individual's personal needs or wants.

Keep in mind that in gift structuring for an individual one gift vehicle may not serve the need. You may need to combine two or more gift vehicles to meet the multiple needs of donors and their families.

How do you determine the needs of the donor and his / her family? This brings us full circle to the very beginning of the marketing plan. Properly carried out chatting and cultivation will get you a considerable amount of information once you have a "suspect." If you have undertaken a good marketing study and developed a good marketing plan, you will have come up with specific target markets and product designs for each of those target markets. You will effectively communicate with specific markets by specifically addressing their concerns and needs. You *will* then get responses because you will be discussing, and helping to solve, a problem, rather than soliciting a gift.

When talking to potential donors, certain situations in conversation will trigger your thoughts about those target markets and the products you designed for them. This is issue spotting. When you hear those certain key issues, the opening will be right to make a suggestion or a proposal to the donor based on a product design for a market segment. At this point it is not an imposition, you are truly meeting a need that you have heard stated. Because you have so thoroughly studied the types of needs and wants in your constituency, you are ready to respond.

If you learn of a situation where, for example, a man is discussing his concern over his grandchildren's college education, it is time to alter your approach. You suggest individual tailoring or gift structuring for the individual (akin to product design for the market segment.) Remember, do not stop marketing before the close, and never stop after the close.

In planned giving circles we quite often speak of "readiness." Readiness is always a concept concerning the organization. However, this concept can be viewed from both sides; the readiness of the donor is just as important as the readiness of the organization. Keep in mind what Peter Drucker said, "Marketing should make selling superfluous."

SECTION THREE

"IMPLEMENT"

Until one is committed, there is hesitancy, the chance to draw back, always ineffectiveness. Concerning all acts of initiative there is one elementary truth the ignorance of which kills countless ideas and endless plans: That the moment one definitely commits oneself then providence moves, too. All sorts of things occur to help one that would never otherwise have occurred. A whole stream of events and meetings and material assistance which no man could have dreamed would come his way. Whatever you can do or dream you can, begin it! Boldness has genius, power, and magic in it.

— W.H. Murray and Goethe
as quoted in *Return to the Alps*,
by Max Knight

5

Working Effectively Within Your Organization

Coming together is a beginning; keeping together is progress; working together is success.

— Henry Ford, *Remarks of Famous People*

Role of the Board

No major program can be effectively established, nor can it succeed, without the board's understanding and support. That is an accepted fact for all types of programs with a corporate body.

A corporation is an artificial legal entity that can act only through its officers and agents. A for-profit corporation generally has a board of directors comprised of both outside and inside directors. That is, some members of the board are also employed in management (inside) and others are brought in from outside endeavors for their knowledge and expertise. This arrangement generally allows the board to have full knowledge of the functioning of the corporation. Officers of the board are often management employees, but the chairman of the board usually is not.

A nonprofit board, on the other hand, is almost always composed of outside directors. They typically serve in a voluntary, unpaid capacity, while for-profit boards are generally paid significant amounts. Nonprofit board members are not always chosen for their management expertise either. Instead, they may be selected on a quota basis representing the organization's constituency, or they may be selected for their standing in the community, their wealth, their profession or their family or business name (visibility and prominence).

With this type of make-up, nonprofit boards are generally ill-equipped to handle their responsibilities. In some cases, members have never served as a corporate director and do not understand their role. On top of that, too few nonprofits have good board training sessions, covering such items as management skills and legal and fiduciary liabilities.

For this, and other reasons, problems often crop up with boards — particularly ineffectiveness — and nonprofit management does not know how to fix them. Sometimes nonprofit management is too timid in solving such problems or ousting board members. In other respects, because the directors have low-level involvement and the staff has all of the information, the staff may dominate and the board will become a rubber-stamp board.

These problems are not conducive to good quality fund raising, especially planned giving, which requires close board involvement. The same is true for capital campaigns.

What is the board's role in general? There are five parts to a board member's role: policy, legal, volunteer, financial and fiduciary. From a policy standpoint, the board is ultimately responsible for the organization's operations and activities. While the board differentiates between policy and daily management, there are no individual decisions. The board acts as a body, through minutes and resolutions of the board. This falls under the quorum requirement.

The board can also appoint committees, but should first determine the scope and purpose of the committee. Often, different committees oversee and help support different aspects of staff activity. It is important for all parties, the board and the staff, to determine and agree on the extent of each other's delegated authority.

From a legal standpoint, a defining rule to follow may be

derived from the California Nonprofit Corporation Law and the law of many other states that have the Uniform Nonprofit Corporation Law. The activities and affairs of a corporation are to be conducted, and all corporate powers exercised, by or under the direction of the board.

The board may delegate the management of the activities of the corporation to any person or persons, management company or committee, however composed, provided that the activities and affairs of the corporation are to be managed and all corporate powers are to be exercised under the ultimate direction of the board.

A director must perform the duties of a director, including duties as a member of any committee of the board upon which the director may serve, in good faith, in a manner that s/he deems to be in the best interests of the corporation and with such care, including reasonable inquiry, as an ordinarily prudent person in a like position would use under similar circumstances.

In performing the duties of a director, a director is entitled to rely on information, opinions, reports or statements, including financial statements and other financial data, in each case prepared or presented by the following:

(1) One or more officers or employees of the corporation whom the director believes to be reliable and competent in the matters presented

(2) Counsel, independent accountants or other persons as to matters which the director believes to be within such person's professional or expert competence

(3) A committee of the board, upon which the director does not serve, as to matters within its designated authority, which committee the director believes to merit confidence, so long as, in any such case, the director acts in good faith, after reasonable inquiry when the need therefore is indicated by the circumstances and without knowledge that would cause such reliance to be unwarranted

Except as provided in any rules against self-dealing, a person who performs the duties of a director, in accordance with the above subdivisions, generally has no liability based upon any alleged failure to discharge the person's obligations as a director.

The board's legal role also includes Standards for Investment or Retention of Assets, which applies to all assets held by the corporation for investment, but not to assets which are directly related to the corporation's public or charitable programs.

In some states, in investing, reinvesting, purchasing, acquiring, exchanging, selling and managing the corporation's investments, the board is obliged to do the following:

(1)   Avoid speculation, look instead to the permanent disposition of the funds, considering the probable income, as well as the probable safety of the corporation's capital.

(2)   Comply with additional standards, if any, imposed by the articles, bylaws or express terms of an instrument or agreement pursuant to which the assets were contributed to the corporation.

Generally, where an investment conforms to these provisions in a gift instrument authorizing such investment, no violation of these rules occurs.

As we said, nonprofit board members are made up of volunteers. Let's look at their role from this standpoint.

In "The Strategy Gap in Not-For-Profits," by Israel Unterman and Richard Hart-Davis, published in the May-June 1982 *Harvard Business Review,* the authors contend that business executives who become trustees of nonprofits too often fail to apply their managerial expertise to their volunteer efforts in not-for-profit organizations — a void that is most apparent in the formulation and implementation of strategy. It asks:

A.   Why is the tool of strategic management so infrequently used, especially by small and medium sized not-for-profits?

B.   How do boards of trustees behave when making strategic decisions?

C.   How does their behavior compare with that of directors of for-profit enterprises?

The answers might lie in the fact that the composition of the board of a nonprofit differs from the board of a for-profit business or institution in six basic ways: (1) nonprofit boards are larger, (2) nonprofits rely on greater use of the executive director, (3) there are fewer inside directors, (4) staff has limited managerial experience, (5) there are fixed terms of service and (6) many trustees ignore the task of discussing policies, accepting the decisions of the executive instead.

Larger boards are often used to satisfy a volunteer's desire for nominal involvement while leaving the director in control. They also often work on nonprofit boards for the public visibility, the business contacts and other social benefits.

According to the *Harvard Business Review* article, inside corporate directors make up approximately forty to fifty percent of for-profit boards. Nonprofit boards, however, generally have no inside corporate directors or they have one who serves as the executive director. Very few nonprofits permit staff members to deal directly with the board. Sometimes boards of directors of nonprofits who deal with staff and learn too much about the operation are viewed as meddlers.

The *Harvard Business Review* study reports the attendance of corporate directors to be at ninety percent or better, whereas the attendance of nonprofit directors ranges between fifty to sixty percent. It also concludes that nonprofit organizations consume more meeting time than for-profit board meetings.

In general a board's key functions in the nonprofit setting include:

A.   Selection of the CEO.
B.   Review of financial performance.
C.   Social considerations of nonprofit corporate activities.
D.   Policies for the organization and procedures to implement them. Fund raising is expected to be an active portion of latter activity. Donations of professional time and personal contributions are expected.

It is more difficult for small nonprofits to attract trustees of considerable experience or wealth. These organizations, then, are more likely to rely on people in business, local professionals, people from the ranks of wage earners and spouses of business people. In this case, the formulation of goals and policies is often relegated to an executive director, who, by virtue of this situation, has the power of both the CEO and the corporate board combined.

Although the financial task is one of the more important board activities, it is rarely indicated to newcomers to the board that they must devote significant time to revenues generated from fund raising. For this reason, an analysis should be performed for board training sessions showing the five potential categories of nonprofit revenue and what percentage of this organization's revenue comes from each of the categories, specifically fund raising. The board should then expect to devote at least the same percentage of time to fund-raising matters as the fund-raising revenue bears to the total revenue. The five categories are:

(1)   Money deriving from the program
(2)   Investment income
(3)   Unrelated businesses
(4)   Gifts from individuals
(5)   Corporate, foundation and government grants

Fund accounting has confused many business-oriented nonprofit directors and has made it difficult for them to acquire the essential information from financial statements on which they must base decisions. Financial accounting standards are becoming more clearly stated and are moving in the direction of reporting on a basis similar to that of for-profit businesses. Several recent FASB pronouncements in accounting have helped.

The last aspect of the director or trustee's role is the fiduciary responsibility Money donated to a charitable organization is considered to be money held in "public trust." The board of directors is expected to handle the money in a way satisfactory to those who donated it. Certain agencies, such as the state Attorney General's office and the IRS, watchdog this fiduciary role of the board of directors of a nonprofit.

As far as the board's role in planned giving is concerned, it is essential that its members understand the program and the need for such a program.

The planned giving business plan should be completed thoroughly and presented to the board with a cover sheet summarizing some of the more pertinent facts. The board needs to understand that the ongoing financial vitality of the organization depends on long-term programs. The key is to coordinate planned giving efforts with the strategic planning undertaken by the board. The need for a planned giving program is akin to saving for retirement.

Above all, a planned giving program requires commitment from a board of directors. What does "commitment" mean? Every article written and every speech given regarding the board's role in planned giving calls for commitment of the board. However, a good definition of board commitment is rather elusive. A board is not born with commitment, it must be developed. That development is incumbent upon the planned giving officer.

Among other things, commitment includes understanding, giving support, both in terms of time and money, and, most important of all, making it one's own project — true involvement in the project.

Motivation is often the key to that commitment. Here are a few motivational tips:

(1)   Have an executive who is excited about planned giving as a long-term project and who is willing to devote time to the development of it. If you do not have this, how did you get hired or assigned?

(2)   Board presentations, typical presentations or seminars to the board are interesting, but perhaps not effective, creatures. Not enough thought or planning is generally put into them. The first obstacle to overcome is the need for adequate time before the board. Too often the planned giving officer is given twenty minutes, which is cut down to ten minutes, which is cut down to five minutes during the board meeting. In fact, a board presentation on either the planned giving program or planned giving vehicles should be the total agenda for

that board meeting, if possible. A consultant may be used for certain types of presentations. Make it fun and not threatening. No board member likes to be reminded that s/he will die and ought to leave a gift behind.

(3)   Quite often organizations plan a board seminar without focusing on *why* the seminar is being presented. The seminar must have a definite purpose to be achieved. For example, the initial board seminar should be one that explains the need for a program, what a program is, how it shall be carried out and what results can be expected by the organization over the long-term. Subsequent board presentations can be motivational rather than explanatory, showing the gift vehicles (educational) or strategy situations (motivational).

(4)   Make a checklist on how to establish commitment.

- Be interested yourself and project the "vision and fervor" of the project.
- Be sensitive to volunteer reaction and adjust to it as you go along.
- Be simple in your presentations — do not waste their valuable time.
- Be persistent — communication is a *process*, not an event; no's often come before yes's.
- Treat your board member or volunteer like a donor — be kind — do not bludgeon him/her with "commitment."

Does this mean every board member must give before a program starts? No, be gentle, and CULTIVATE COMMITMENT as you would a contribution. Nurture the relationship. Do not demand gifts; make people want to give.

Just as philanthropy has to be voluntary, so does commitment. A process of cultivation towards commitment is essential in developing the board's interest in the new planned giving program. It is necessary to get them engaged in some way, even a very minor way like reviewing papers, having lunch, answering a question for you. Be resourceful.

Remember that it is also important to use board members in line with their personality traits and what they enjoy. Enlisting a board member to do a task s/he does not enjoy — like soliciting — may result in the loss of a person who may have been very valuable to the organization in another function. Either the board member will become soured on the organization as a whole, or s/he will avoid working for the planned giving effort.

In most cases, board members and volunteer committees get to know one another and the executive fairly well. The process of gentle interrogation of the executive and chairman of the board regarding these personality traits and interests will result in placing volunteers in one of the following six boxes, which are categories providing an assessment of a volunteer's best use.

1. List Maker Person who knows a lot about other people in your particular community and can help in identifying prospects and completing prospect files.	**2. Good Contact/Influence** Person who knows a lot of other people in the community and can identify those with influence. Then the "matchmakers" can tell if any of these people can be matched with the prospects.
3. Matchmaker Person who knows who, knows who is, knows who owes who favors, who is seen at parties and dinners together, etc. This person can help *match the best donor openers and solicitors to each prospect.*	**4. Door Opener** Person who can invite prospects to lunches, events, etc. and generally cultivate a prospect so that you can ultimately ask for the gift.
5. Solicitor Person who is able and willing to ask for the gift.	**6. Gift Maker** Person capable of and willing to make gifts.

The volunteer may then be approached to undertake certain functions within those boxes on a limited basis. From this effort, the volunteer may find him/herself fascinated by the program or interested in what s/he is doing. One may even wish to take on a little bit more.

In fact, at some point in the process when a reluctant board member sees the progress of the program, s/he may even decide to get *very* involved or even make a contribution.

To this end, consider signing a "board treaty" that solidifies the duties and responsibilities of the board, as well as determines your limits of authority as a planned giving officer.

The board treaty is an understanding between the board (or CEO) and the planned giving department as to what will be undertaken, in what time frame and how evaluations will be made. It is important that the board understand the rationale behind having a board treaty. It is primarily for the purpose of getting through the really tough times during the organizational stage of the planned giving project. It is one of the early things you must work on with the board in planned giving — getting them to understand that there will be a "treaty" and that you do expect them to sign it (once it is to their liking as well as to yours).

There is something about putting things in writing that makes a goal, project or program more tangible and attainable. It defines the process, maps the plan and identifies the important players and their specific roles. It solidifies commitment.

The first important step in creating a board treaty is to sell your boss on the idea of having one. If your boss hired you, s/he will look bad if you do not succeed, but s/he will look great when you do. Use this concept to prove the necessity of your boss's involvement in structuring your board treaty. The following is an example of such a treaty:

Board Treaty

The Board of Directors ("Board") of _____ has undertaken the creation and implementation of a planned giving program to cultivate, solicit and bring to fruition gifts of a long-range nature to ensure the long-term vitality of _____. This program, having never before been undertaken, will require considerable effort, time and expense before it becomes revenue-producing. Nevertheless, the Board believes it is in the best interests of _____ to undertake the program. The Planned Giving Officer has presented to the Board a summary and a detailed chronology of tasks for the first twelve months of the program and a projection of activities for the following twelve months. Because the Planned Giving Officer believes s/he needs to be granted the opportunity to follow this chronology to succeed in creating the Planned Gifts Program, we have been asked to agree to certain terms and conditions:

Agreements by Board

1. The activities of organization and preparation of a planned gifts program are often mistaken by others as inactivity or lack of success, especially when placed in an environment of short-term goals and yearly fund-raising cycles. The Board agrees to view planned giving as separate from short-term funding cycles and to be aware that time is needed for internal organization and planning.

2. The manner of cultivation of planned gift donors is considerably different and longer than that for existing programs. The Board agrees to permit, and accept, the time factor in planned gift cultivation; it will not place undue pressure on the Planned Giving Officer to close planned gifts if the donor in question has not finalized his/her financial planning.

3. The Board understands that its own commitment, in terms of time and involvement, is critical to the success of planned giving. It agrees to provide that time and involvement on a reasonable basis, providing access to the Planned Gifts Officer and providing responses to questions or decisions presented by the Planned Gifts Program.

4. The Board agrees to commit funds over the next thirty-six months for the start-up of this endeavor possibly without realizing returns. It agrees to review the proposed budget and not unreasonably withhold funding necessary to the success of the program.

5. The Board understands that new categories of expenses will be involved, including, but not limited to, attorneys' and consultants' fees.

6. The Board agrees to evaluate the Planned Giving Officer based on the goals and tasks set forth in the Summary Chronology and its accompanying Evaluation Techniques, as opposed to monetary goals, for the first thirty-six months.

7. The Board will not permit the imposition by itself or others of monetary goals in lieu of the stated objectives and tasks during the first thirty-six months.

8. The Board agrees to learn planned giving techniques and cases necessary to gaining a better understanding of the program and areas in which the Board may be of assistance.

Agreements by Planned Giving Officer

1. The Planned Giving Officer ("Officer") agrees to adhere to the Detailed Chronology to the best of his/her ability and in good faith.

2. The Officer agrees to report, in a timely fashion, the problems that occur in following the Chronology to the Development Director, the Executive Director or the Chairman of the Board.

3. The Officer agrees to use budgeted funds wisely and only for those items whose objective is to generate future revenue for the organization.

3. The Officer agrees to use budgeted funds wisely and only for those items whose objective is to generate future revenue for the organization.

4. The Officer agrees to undertake self-study to perfect his/her skills, in addition to any training or seminars funded by_____. The Officer further agrees to share knowledge so gained with the staff and volunteers of _____. The Officer agrees to use such knowledge for the advancement of the program to the revenue-

5. The Officer agrees to do everything reasonable to try to achieve long-term employment in order to succeed in long-term donor cultivation. The Officer agrees to make that cultivation "programmatic" (available to all and recorded properly) as opposed to "individualize" (that which the

The Chairman of the Board agrees to sign and present this Treaty to the full Board at a regular meeting of the Board of Directors for corporate resolution to enact these provisions. The Treaty is to be included with the regular Minutes of the Corporation.

_____   _____
Date   Planned Giving Officer

_____   _____
Date   Chairman of the Board

Corporate resolution undertaken at the Board Meeting dated _____ and entered into the Minutes thereof.

_____
Secretary

Meet with the board chairman and/or key members to introduce a draft like this and request their comments. Revise the draft along the lines of those comments, then meet with an expanded group of board members, either as a group or individually, to sell them on the concept, using a consultant if necessary.

When a substantial number of board members are in agreement, ask that the chairman of the board sign it and present it at a board meeting where it can be read. The corporate body can resolve to accept this board treaty, and have it signed and put in the minutes.

Developing a treaty is an effective tool for a planned giving officer because some nonprofit organizations tend to keep board members distant from staff. While there may be acceptable reasons for this distance concerning other parts of the program, access to board members is vital to the success of the planned giving program.

The executive director, the chairman of the board and the planned giving officer should meet to discuss access to board members and introductions to them at a very early stage in the chronology. Ongoing communications of various sorts with board members are necessary because, according to your treaty, board members will be solicitors and will help turn up various leads. In addition, ongoing communication with board members will draw them closer to the project and will create more involvement over the long haul.

Within this process, the planned giving department should supply the board with a clear indication of what it is committing to in terms of dollar amounts expended to get this project off the ground. The budget demonstrates that the board must be willing to spend money in order to get the project going, just as it would cost money to start a new business which is ultimately expected to undertake lucrative activities.

The board must be shown that in order to succeed in this project, it needs to be committed to maintaining the planned giving program *until that program produces more than it costs.*

Eventually, the cost/benefit ratio of planned giving will be very attractive. But, in all fairness, the board must understand up front what it is undertaking. For this reason, a proposed, detailed one-year budget, as previously outlined, and two following years of proforma proposed budgets are the minimum requirements needed to show the board its commitment in dollar terms. It will help to gather information from other organizations as to their start-up costs for such a program.

In addition to these budgets, the planned giving officer must provide a report to the board at least once every six months. The report should be written and briefly include accomplished tasks, prospects seen and any interesting gift structures proposed to those prospects. It should also entail a six-month prospective list of objectives to be achieved, including further tasks and other prospects to be seen. It should report on the status of a budget projected on a yearly basis, and include a budget report which should show six-month year-to-date figures. It should list any outstanding proposals or prospects — with suggested structures — and it should specifically request the board's help, in case board members happen to know the prospect involved.

Each report should be designed to keep the board members involved without overworking them. To be certain members of your planned giving policy committee are receiving and reading this report, return forms or signature lines should be included as well.

You *should* ask that all written reports be initialed and returned to you at least from the CEO and your committees. The more they respond the better covered you are if the board or the executive wonders if, in fact, you are adequately fulfilling your function of preparing a planned giving program. In other words, keep everybody informed at all stages. Initialing provides assurance that your reports have at least been seen, including your requests for further help. Before many gifts are in, it is hard for everyone to tell if you are doing a good job or not.

It should be understood that every organization faces the possibility that certain board members are not functioning to their fullest commitment. Organizations deal with this problem in various ways.

Some typical problems planned giving persons have with board members include: the inactive or inefficient board member; a chairman who is against planned giving; the absentee board member who has money, but you never see him/her (and maybe s/he does not give either).

While it is a very difficult and delicate situation, there are ways to suggest board turnover. Although this may sound like a drastic measure, it must be considered because you need active board members for your program to succeed.

If fewer than ten percent of your board members are ineffective, you probably do not need to worry about this question. But, if more than a quarter or a third of your board fits in the inactive category, the inefficient category or the other categories listed above, you need to determine whether you can turn them into active participating members. If not, you should speak with the executive director or the chairman of the board about why board involvement in fund raising is essential (using the ideas listed in this section so far). Then, politely but frankly, suggest removal of certain board members. This action is made much easier if you have already prepared and gotten board signatures on your treaty.

Planned Giving Policies

Much confusion exists about planned giving policies and guidelines. It is simple. Policies are board policies adopted to protect the entity, its board and its management from legal exposure. Guidelines are to help staff, consultants and volunteers do their job. That much said, let us address *topics* to discuss in order to write your policies and guidelines. DO NOT COPY SOMEONE ELSE'S. It is like wearing someone else's shoes or clothes. It will rarely fit. Think through your own.

Much havoc can be wreaked by loose-lipped staff members or volunteers, which may seriously jeopardize donor relations. One important policy is confidentiality about donors and assets.

A statement of confidentiality is a statement from the board, designed to filter down to all persons dealing with donor information. Each member of the team involved in fund raising, whether it be staff or volunteer, should be asked to read and sign the policy statement regarding confidentiality. To allay their fears, it should be made clear that this is not an oath; however, it is an understanding that all persons are on the same "wavelength" regarding donor records. Following is a sample policy statement.

Policy Regarding Confidentiality

All records maintained by [this organization] relevant to our donors are strictly confidential. This information is not made available to the public for any purpose, unless prior written consent is given by the donor.

Certain restricted groups will have access to certain information, as is required to achieve the legitimate fundraising objectives of [organization]. Donor records which are not related to the purposes of these groups will not be accessible.

Groups with limited access to donor records are:
Chairman of Board of Directors
President of [organization]
Chairman of Development Committee
Planned Gifts Committee
Annual gifts Committee
Corporate/Foundation Gifts Committee
Director of Finance Administration
Development Director
Planned Giving Director
Development Assistants

All [organization's] staff are aware of this policy regarding confidentiality. Volunteer fundraisers are cautioned to use the information only for fundraising purposes and are urged to respect the confidentiality of this information, as well.

Whether or not the organization serves as trustee of charitable trusts, it has a fiduciary responsibility and it should understand the nature of the fiduciary role and should resolve to accept such fiduciary responsibility in the corporate minutes.

A planned giving staff member should make a study of what fiduciary responsibility is, and prepare a summary report for the board. Based on this report, a corporate resolution can be formed. The following is a sample corporate resolution:

Corporate Resolution

WHEREAS, the Board of Directors of _____ has determined to manage, as trustee or in other capacity, gifts in the forms of [trusts], [pooled income funds], [life insurance policies], [gift annuities], and

WHEREAS, it has been apprised of the responsibilities of acting in such fiduciary capacity as outlined in the attached memorandum,

BE IT RESOLVED THAT the Board of Directors of _____ accepts such fiduciary responsibility and will exercise its fiduciary role in a manner designed to protect and guard the interests of the beneficiaries named in such gift vehicles.

_____   _____
Date   Secretary

The board of directors should also understand the ethical considerations of running a planned giving program. We will delve further into this issue in chapter 8, but we will touch on it here to say that each organization must address its ethics policy and prepare a statement to be adopted by the board which will lay the foundation for the organization's relationship to the outside world with regard to major gifts/planned gifts. This is necessary both for legal liability and for "media liability."

There also must be a policy regarding serving as trustee. New, broad exposure to liability results from a nonprofit serving

as a trustee of its donors' trusts. The board must confront these issues before deciding to act as a trustee.

The board must consider its policy regarding hazardous
waste as well. Real estate liability for hazardous waste has become
phenomenally expensive. The EPA does not care if you are a nonprofit. It will force you to pay the costs of clean-up if waste is
found. Therefore, strict policies, and then procedures, for review
and acceptance of real estate must be established.

Every organization should consider certain things as part of
planned giving policies. These policies should be drafted by the
staff members based on items that are important to daily operation,
but may need decision after board discussion and vote.

Traditional planned giving guidelines, that people copy out of
books, are often made the subject of committee process by organizations. This is a waste of time and effort on the part of volunteers
when their efforts would be better used for either technical or marketing advice, or in prospecting. Consideration and drafting by the
staff is more efficient. It can then be presented to the volunteer committee, to selected board members or to the board for approval.

Following is a list of some items you should consider for your
policies:

(1)   Use of Committees
        Should planned giving committees be comprised of
        board members only or partly board members and
        partly other volunteers to carry out planned giving
        functions? Should any committee exist with no board
        members?
(2)   Creation of Endowments; Spending Policy
        Has the board resolved to accept and hold endow-
        ment funds? True endowment and/or quasi-endow-
        ment? Will all the income therefrom be spent? Some?
        Any capital gain? Realized, unrealized? Guidelines
        should be developed with the investment committee.
        If there is no board resolution, make this a board poli-
        cy issue.
(3)   Conflicts of Interest
        In what situations might a conflict occur? Is it differ-

ent for board, volunteers, staff? What if someone derives economic benefit for him/herself?

(4)   Fiduciary Responsibilities (See also Resolution above)
Will donee act as trustee of its charitable remainder trusts? Will it handle its own PIF? If it issues gift annuities, will it reinsure them? Once these board decisions are made, guidelines on their implementation will be necessary.

(5)   Use of Outside Counsel
Establish guidelines to provide when a question of legal or estate planning nature should be referred to outside counsel, particularly to avoid the impression that the organization is engaging in the unauthorized practice of law for its donors.

(6)   Types of Property Acceptable/Gift Acceptance Procedures
Consider the types of property for both outright and deferred gifts that you will accept: e.g., real estate (where and how it will be reviewed for marketability, the procedure for reviewing for hazardous waste, indemnifications from donor on hazardous waste), personal property (what is and is not acceptable — jewelry, computers, etc.), limited partnership interests and the like.

(7)   Confidentiality (See also Policy Regarding Confidentiality)
The Board should adopt a policy that states that donor records and solicitations are to remain confidential and accessible to the smallest number of staff and volunteers. Then staff guidelines must delineate how to implement the policy.

(8)   No Engagement in Gift-Giving Schemes or Scams that May Threaten Either Public Image or Exempt Status; No Unreasonable Finders Fees
The various tax shelters related to charitable giving should be avoided and finders fees should not generally be paid. Guidelines on how to handle these situations are needed.

(9)   Maintenance of Gift Records and Accounting
      The long-term maintenance of a donor's restriction
      or intent must be made a clear policy for future
      boards and staff. A gift that matures in twenty or
      twenty-five years might arrive at the donee's office
      after those concerned with its transfer have gone.
      State Attorneys General nevertheless require exact
      administration. Therefore, a direction must be set for
      the finance and administration department.

(10) Annual Report on Planned Giving Funds, also sent to
      Beneficiaries
      Although perhaps not required by accounting princi-
      ples, an annual report of each donor's fund and all
      funds combined should be considered. Certain state
      laws may require beneficiary reports.

(11) Statement of Ethics
      Questions of ethics and undue influence must be ad-
      dressed, whether by board or staff or both.

Keep in mind that policies are not rules. They are intended to
foresee and forestall problems.

Use of Committees

We have talked about committees that spring from boards,
and the characteristics that often seem to stunt their effectiveness.
Many times board committees are too mixed — financial professionals, board members, knitters, socialites. Or, they are too unfo-
cused. They have no clear idea of why they are there. On top of
these difficulties their participation is often forced, and rarely includes training. This, of course, sends the serious business-types
packing because they feel their time is being wasted. High turnover will continue until these problems are solved. Sure, committees can be fun at times, but ultimately it is a job with goals to
achieve.

One way to avoid or correct these dangerous routines is to

break the committees up into focused groups made up of members with expertise or interest in each area. For example, rather than one committee tackling policy, marketing and technical aspects of planned giving, establish three separate committees or subcommittees for each area.

A policy committee is comprised of board members and/or other volunteers. Their job is to help you set policy, scope, perhaps a budget and to work with prospects.

A marketing committee is composed of marketing professionals. Their job is to help with a marketing plan, help with effective communications and help with contacts with the media.

A technical committee is composed of financial professionals. Their job is to help with technical questions and structures (but not in the nature of ongoing legal advice, for which you should pay) and to leverage out into the financial community for you.

Let us further examine the make-up and role of each. Consider the function of a policy committee. Its definition is to work with staff to develop plans for the program; to set necessary policies; to develop, cultivate and solicit prospects; to identify the core group and form the initial matrix, then to contact, cultivate, structure gifts and solicit those prospects; to identify and reach expanded markets, participate in mailings, analyze returns, then cultivate, etc.; to participate in donor seminars; and to help draft, refine and update a planned giving case statement.

The same six-box approach we outlined earlier in this chapter should be used in the selection of a committee. The committee should be composed of seven, nine or more volunteers. There will be turnover. The committee should have at least some board members; others should be well acquainted with the program and the constituents. The members should be invited by the chairman of the board or an officer. This committee should be selected fairly early. It will take time to consider the right mix.

The committee members should also be educated about or trained to fulfill their role. The nature of the "ask" is first and foremost in such training. Fill them in on the discovery process and what to do if someone tells them "no."

Give them an explanation of the vehicles, perhaps by using

case studies. Demonstrate the process and what it includes:

- Use of contacts / getting in the door
- Meeting face-to-face
- Chat
- Organizational "hot issues"
- How the prospect is involved
- Needs of organization
- Needs of prospect
- Suggested structure
- Prospect reaction
- Ask

Educate them on:

- How many meetings may be required
- How not to avoid dollar levels up front
- Having meetings with no mention of fund raising to catch up on the organization's important matters
- Not denying the underlying fund-raising motive

Explain why staff members must be able to contact volunteers. Make sure they understand the necessity of accepting responsibility for the job. It really is a job.

Motivate committee members. They must get feedback, thanks and recognition from important people in the organization. They must see the progress, even if it is slight.

But, do not burn them out by overuse. Keep phone calls and letters short and succinct — PREPARE BEFORE CONTACTING — wasting their time will undermine motivation.

Let's consider the marketing committee and define its function, which is to help create an effective marketing plan, to advise on markets and target markets, to advise on designing effective communications to reach those markets, to help develop new markets, to aid in public relations and media matters and to work with gift structures from the technical committee for effective communication methods and designs.

This should be a five or six-person committee. Its members

should be made up of communications experts — from marketing, advertising, public relations, the newspaper or broadcast media. None need to be board members. Some acquaintance with the organization is helpful, but not a prerequisite.

Staff members or board members may invite the new committee member, depending upon "rank" in his/her profession, ego considerations, amount of time requested, etc. This committee should be set up very early.

Their training should include an explanation of philanthropy, the process of obtaining funds, what is written on nonprofit marketing, how planned giving helps an organization, how planned giving marketing is different from marketing the nonprofit program, the gift vehicles, gift situations, case histories and who is doing what in development marketing. It should also include an introduction to the industry and to the organization.

The committee members also need motivation — feedback, thanks and recognition in their own journals or circles. They need to see the progress in the marketing plan, the possibility of breaking new ground in this business and the opportunity for new business of their own. Bring them to events and on tours, take them to lunch on the premises and have them meet the board chairman and others.

The technical committee is defined in the following manner: to meet with a staff person to discuss gift strategies, to help keep the development staff educated on important issues regarding donors' assets, to be available for the unusual questions within their disciplines, to work with the target markets that the marketing committee develops in structuring gift opportunities, to leverage contacts in the financial community and to help prepare/present seminars for donors.

This committee should be fairly large, perhaps ten to fifteen people or maybe more. The members should include lawyers, CPAs, life insurance agents, trust officers, stockbrokers, financial planners, real estate brokers and investment advisors/money managers.

None need to be board members, but board members should be welcome to participate in this capacity. Financial professionals on the board should invite these persons to become committee members. If there are no financial professionals on the board, board members or staff members may invite them. This committee may be set up a little later in the chronology.

The members' training should include philanthropy in general, philanthropy in this industry and philanthropy in this organization. Their training should also include an explanation of the process of obtaining funds, where planned giving fits, the difficulty of gaining access to sufficient donor information for planning, the reluctance of many advisors (and theories as to why), how financial professionals can retain clients/make money in the planned giving area and the gift vehicles and gift structures using examples of all types of assets.

They also need feedback, thanks and recognition in their own journals and circles. They need to see an exciting new structure to use with their own clients, how to gain new business/markets through this volunteer work and actual gifts made (thankful clients, donees).

Have lunch on the premises with these members. Bring them to events and on tours so they become involved and perhaps emotionally invested. Have them meet the board chairman and others.

Meetings for all of these committees should be regularly scheduled, but not too often. The agenda and support materials should be mailed to members at least seven days in advance. The chairman of the committee should meet with staff members in advance for a briefing. Make sure you have a real reason for meeting, not just to "make-work." Run the meeting efficiently and *end on time*. Meet at the organization from time to time while the "program" is in full operation.

Again, it is natural for turnover to occur. Do not keep members who cannot devote time — it is a part-time job. Do not burn bridges when "firing" a committee member — have the full committee make the decision and one person "voted" to do the job. Therefore, no one person is to blame, it saves face and hard feelings. Have a list of alternates ready from the start.

In thanking and giving recognition to these members, remember to be generous but not overbearing. Make it meaningful in a way the committee member will appreciate. Because public recognition may be wonderful or embarrassing, gauge each member's personality and be consistent with all members.

Working with Related Offices

Now let us turn back to your more personnel intensive tasks as a planned giving officer. In assessing current procedures of funds administration for your organization, you may have to invade some past territory.

It is necessary to study exactly what gifts have been processed by the organization to date and the procedures that were followed to attain those gifts. Study any written procedures and the gift flow of the organization, then chart it. If there are no written procedures, write them jointly with the business office. Develop a list of assets the organization knows how to handle and assets that are unfamiliar. Determine whether trusts are/were managed in-house. Assess the technical knowledge of business office staff members regarding planned gifts.

It is necessary to be diplomatic about your invasion into funds administration. You need to explain, or have a consultant explain, the ins and outs of planned gift vehicles, reporting, valuations, dealing with the IRS, unrelated business income, Chapter 42 rules, etc. Then explain to board members, and perhaps to other staff members, the new program to be undertaken. Explain that you do not expect them to be born with this knowledge, but assure them they can learn.

Invite the funds administration staff to your monthly staff meetings. Meet with their committee to outline their committee's role in planned giving and to create in-house training seminars if the funds administration staff is large enough to warrant them.

Train them in fund raising in general. From there, explain vehicles thoroughly. Supply them with all the necessary reporting forms. Create work flows and checklists, cross-checks with development and forms to be used by all offices — gift memoranda. Send the funds administration staff members to outside seminars that you have selected (because you have better access to the field and its information). Send them regular updates gleaned from newsletters and journals regarding rulings, cases and legislation that may affect their end of the process. Go to lunch with them regularly and get to know their concerns.

Communication is the key to an effective and cooperative working situation. Some conflicts are inevitable, others can be avoided. Too often the development office negotiates a gift and then "dumps" it on funds administration. If the funds administration staff then finds it cannot handle the gift as negotiated and/or promised to the donor, tension results. That is why it is important that a negotiation process be set-up to deal with unusual gifts.

This process should involve a vehicle-by-vehicle and asset-by-asset study. The funds administration and planned giving staff members must meet to go through each possible gift arrangement (generic) in advance to see if any problems might arise in light of the expertise of each. They should also discuss how situations will be handled if problems do arise. Would an outside attorney or accountant be brought in? If so, whose budget will cover it?

Set up a procedure for the cases you cannot agree upon. Determine who will decide whether a gift will be made, modified or forgotten.

With that covered, let us determine how to price planned gift opportunities. Hopefully, endowment fund prices are already established. If not, decisions need to be made on what funds to create, how much it costs to support the activity yearly, how much can be earned in the market and whether the gift should cover the entire amount or some portion.

If the gift is deferred, decide how to calculate what the corpus will be worth at the end of life expectancy. Then determine how to project the cost of the project over the same time period. Guidelines will need to be drawn as a result of these projections, and donors will be informed.

Deferred gifts do not become usable for many years. Nevertheless, at the date of gift, the donor may restrict usage to a particular program or geographic area. State law and common law may also require that restrictions be followed. This is why impeccable record-keeping and the flow of information from the development department to funds administration is so important. How will such information be kept intact for the funds administration department that will exist twenty to twenty-five years from now? Fund books and microfiche are just two options, but it is essential that copies be made of pertinent language and/or the whole gift instrument.

Periodically, funds administration should open its records to an audit of deferred gift vehicles and their management to serve as an annual or I-annual check-up. Often a CPA and outside auditors have little knowledge of deferred giving and bless the state of affairs without a true analysis. Here is a suggestion — call in a specialist (even more rare than attorneys with charitable giving knowledge). When you are really up and running, you should have as a reference *After the Gift is Closed*, by Lynda S. Moerschbaecher, to be published by Precept Press, which will cover all aspects of post-gift administration.

Make sure you also take time to consider your relationship with the public relations office. In working with the PR department, it is often necessary to educate the staff members on fund raising. Sometimes the public relations office has its own agenda and does not understand the needs or time frame of fund raising. It may even see fund raising as something other than an integral part of the organization's program. That attitude has to be adjusted.

Invite the PR staff to monthly staff meetings and make a special effort to get them to see the excitement of planned gifts. They generally have a "motivational" type of personality and are likely to respond to something new and creative.

Invite them to donor seminars to see the people you are trying to reach. Ask that one high-level staff person be named to your marketing committee to get them actively involved and more knowledgeable on the process. Provide them with materials from other organizations as well.

Once PR has some knowledge of your program, include them early in your planning stage — using brochures, newsletters and seminars — and be specific about your requests. Make sure the head of the department knows what your marketing committee is doing, and perhaps ask one volunteer to join this committee. The more information you feed them about *what* you are doing and what you hope to achieve, the better they can and will serve you.

Often the in-house PR department is very busy and behind on schedules, so set priorities with them. If you have a mailing, a year-end piece for example, timing is crucial. What if PR says they just cannot get to it? Establish adjudication procedures with the executive before you ever run into a problem. PR can be quite a help, but not when you do not get along.

If you do not like what the PR department has done for you, call in the marketing committee — that is why you have a marketing committee. Have the committee's chairman meet with the PR department head only in necessary cases that cannot be otherwise corrected.

Planned Giving Staffing

Who "does planned giving?" A planned gift program can only be operated by a donee institution that receives gifts in the form of planned gifts. However, anyone, such as planned gift program staff members, major gift staff members or outside advisors (allied professionals), can engage in creating planned gifts and making asset transfers through them. Therefore, it is correct to say that anyone can "do planned giving" in the latter sense. But the program can only be started and sustained by a charitable donee that has learned how to succeed at it.

Staffing for the program can include several models showing who gets the work done, such as:

A.   Executive does planned giving part-time along with everyone else.

B.   Director of development does external relations, PR, development and planned giving.

C.   Director of development does only fund raising, but planned giving is part of the program as well as all other types of fund raising.

D.   Part-time planned giving consultant serves almost as

a staff planned giving officer.

E.   Part-time planned giving staff member serves as an employee devoted only to planned giving.

F.   Full-time planned giving staff member (one) is devoted to planned giving only.

G.   Full-time planned giving staff members (multiple) are devoted to planned giving only, but each person may only conduct a specified portion of the overall planned gift activities.

Whoever does it, certain tasks are inevitably necessary to planned giving despite how many people perform them (or do not perform them). The following chart depicts the essential roles, whether being carried out by a part-time planned giving staff member or many planned giving personnel.

Director of Planned Giving

Support, clerical and financial   Solicitor / Fundraiser   Legal   Gift Admin   Marketing

This can involve a daunting amount of work and skills. Some organizations, therefore, go outside to get extra help, especially at the outset. All organizations have three concerns — monetary / budgetary, staff time allocable to planned giving and use of volunteers. The use of volunteers varies, often inversely, with the list above of who does planned giving. In other words, the less time the staff person has, the more volunteer time is needed. So, the executive also doing planned giving will use volunteers more than the program with multiple planned giving personnel.

Task detailing will show you that planned activities are numerous and continual. It really requires some concerted effort to achieve success. Here is an example of a task detailing we did for a client. This client has an unusually high return on "warm" mailings, ten to twenty percent. It is usually more like five percent. Considering that, take a look at the amount of work a simple bequest mailing can cause:

Sample of Task Detailing
One Bequest Mailing Planning Giving – Bequest Program

Mailings
— 2,500 known supporters, 10-20
     percent return   250-500
— 5,000 others, .5-1 percent return   25-50
Total returns to be processed   275-550

Process:
  (1) Organize returns   1 month
  (2) Correspond with returns   2-3 weeks
  (3) Phone to returns
        3 tries per return, assume 500 returns,
        10 calls per day   30 weeks
  (4) Visits at 10 percent, 50 visits at 2½ weeks   20 weeks
  (5) Follow-up correspondence 1 hour
        per visit   1½ weeks
  (6) Fill in donor data base   1½ weeks
  (7) Proposals to 10 prospects   1½ to 3 weeks
  (8) Proposal follow-up, work with
        donor, attorney or advisor   unpredictable
  (9) Loop back through returns
 (10) New mailing
 (11) Continual work with identified prospects

As to the use of volunteers to help out with all this work, ask who is available, what is the cost of recruiting, do they understand the role of planned giving and have they been trained in how to "ask," for example, do they understand at least the basics:

Identification
- Use of information, reports
- Capability, inclination of donors and the difference between the two
  - generally
  - specifically as to this organization
- Profile of a donor/prospect
- Giving history of the donor

Cultivation
- Meetings, calls (without solicitation)
- Organizational information and gift opportunities available, including cost
- Chat
- Evaluation of interest
- Knowing organizational trends, plans and hot topics

Solicitation
- In-person contact
- Designed product(s) for target market
- Ability to tailor product to individual
- Written proposals

In terms of working with staff and volunteers as a team, within or overseeing development staff, it is important to establish what is called an employment "understanding." Much the way the board treaty outlines board members' duties and responsibilities toward planned giving, the development officer and staff would be wise to establish their own understandings.

Whether oral or written, the development team should set up a game plan that will work. It will not work, however, unless each team member understands the strategy, the outcome and their role in the process.

Because the fruit of planned giving's labor is not immediately realized, the ideal employment term for this team should be no less than five years. That may seem like a long time, but if you look at the job of planned giving as a massive project or, as we have said, even as a small business, the program is likely to just be hitting its stride by the fifth year. Even if your program is going gangbusters ahead of schedule, the process of smoothly transitioning the program into another's hands is a long and delicate one.

In negotiating a salary for the officer and staff members, be sure to consider bonuses and merit increases (find out who will review). Remember also that titles matter. Just like your treaty with the board, find out where your authority begins and ends, then make sure your title reflects that authority.

Do not take your benefits lightly either. Consider:

- medical (self and others)
- dental (self and others)
- disability (self and others)
- life insurance
- retirement plan
- home, apartment, mortgage help
- car
- staff education

Think about expenses and reimbursements:

- travel (what class?)
- entertainment (limitations)
- meals on the road
- phone calls (home and office)
- moving expenses

Be sure you achieve an understanding about your work habits and personnel. Consider your time in the office and on outside calls. Will you need a secretary (part-time or full-time)? Will you seek membership in clubs or associations for the benefit of donors? Will you need consulting time? Will you possess hire-fire capability?

Discuss and determine the budgetary process. Will you:

A.   Work within a given budget?
B.   Help prepare the budget and, if so, with whom?
C.   Set your own budget? Who reviews the budget?

Assess your computer access and your ability to purchase equipment (including software) according to your needs. Are your reporting lines clearly laid out? Is there a process for resolution of disputes regarding employment? Is there an opportunity for you or the staff to gain further education at the organization's expense?

If amendments are needed to your agreement or understanding, who must participate in them? Are they to be in writing or not?

If you develop a major employment conflict, would you receive a notice of termination? After employment is terminated would you be given recommendations, the use of a secretary and letterhead and out-placement help? If you are the one terminating an employee, where do these issues fall in your policy?

The more "understanding" that is forged at the outset, the better you and your program will operate within the organization.

6

Working Outside the Organization

Everything comes to him who hustles while he waits.
— Thomas Alva Edison, *Words of Wisdom to Live By*

It is generally understood that most nonprofits looking to bring gifts inside the program must go outside the organization to gain them. Many officers of planned giving programs, however, are slow to take advantage of the true resources that can help lead them to such gifts. Long before donor or professional seminars are set up, there is leg work to do and contact to be made.

Working with Financial Professionals

In approaching your community, whether geographic or non-geographic, think about the various contacts in the outside financial world and how they might be able to help you. Consider financial advisors, such as:

- Trust officers
- Lawyers
- CPAs
- Life insurance agents/CLUs
- Financial planners
- Stock brokers
- Real estate brokers/agents
- Investment counsel/money managers
- Casualty insurance agents

In essence, this group of professionals is a market in itself, a leveraged market. Each of them is connected in some way to potential donors. Each of them has some level of control over people and assets, whether simply to make a suggestion or strongly advise.

A trust officer is employed by the trustee who owns the title to property held for beneficiaries according to the trust document. While the trust officer has no real control over the person who set up the trust, s/he often wields great influence with trustors and beneficiaries. Trust officers are like salespeople, in that they are constantly in the field making new contacts with people who are planning to sell property or a business, or who are in various other situations that might lead to a charitable gift. Get to know trust officers and have them introduce you to people they too are looking to help. You can be of mutual benefit to one another. Every trust officer I know is a friendly sort.

Attorneys can be a tremendous help or a tremendous obstacle to planned giving. Many of them are not familiar with planned gifts. They do, however, greatly influence the action of their clients. Help them to understand the process. Get them accept certain gift structures and ease their concerns with the opportunities of planned giving. As time goes on in this field, more attorneys are becoming knowledgeable about and open to the uses of charitable tools in planning.

Certified Public Accountants (CPAs) are very influential when it comes to their clients. Of all of the advisors, this is the one that people are actually controlled by. If a CPA says, "Don't do it, it is not good for you," your donor most likely will not. Work hard to meet with them one-on-one to explain the options of planned gifts. Do not hesitate to call them. Be sure to set a time limit to show them you will not take too much of their time. If you tell them you will only need fifteen minutes, stick to it. Follow-up with a letter and brochure, but do not overwhelm them with marketing material.

Life insurance agents are involved with individual estate planning, which is always a target market for planned gifts. Casualty insurance brokers are in-the-know when it comes to upcoming business sales or transactions. Find ways to meet with these people, get to know them and share information.

Financial planners, business brokers and stock brokers are money managers who also have a lot of control over their clients financial actions. Because many planned gifts come by way of real estate, get to know real estate agents as well. Try to get invited to make a presentation at one of their strategic seminars. Let agents know how planned giving can help their business. Show them just a few real estate techniques, but do not cover everything. Business brokers are basically an untapped source of potential referrals. The people they represent are those looking to sell their businesses. What better contact could you make?

These are the types of business professionals you want to have regular contact with them. Make friends, and nurture and cultivate these contacts. Try to send business their way when you can. Remember, it is a two-way street. However, be careful, and clear that you are not endorsing specific individuals or guaranteeing the outcome of the work when making recommendations. Find ways to thank them as well; for example, if one is particularly helpful to your program, perhaps a notice in their professional journal honoring their volunteer work.

In appealing to these professionals, take into account their form of compensation. Understanding the way in which one is paid helps to set a particular mentality about one's work. It also sets the tone between advisor and client. Their compensation is classified in three basic forms:

(1)   Staff (on salary) — Trust officers (profit center)
(2)   Hourly — Lawyers, CPAs and some financial planners

(3)   Commission — Life and casualty insurance, financial
       planners, stock brokers, real estate agents and invest-
       ment counsel, business brokers

Realizing the way in which these professionals are paid
helps you determine not only the process of their work and the degree of their involvement, but the relationship with their clients —
their degree of influence and control. Fear of a loss of business if a
charitable gift is made needs to be addressed differently in each
case. If your attempt at getting a gift from their client means the
professional loses immediate or ongoing business, they will not
participate. If, on the other hand, your proposed gift or your program brings more business to them, you will have an enduring relationship. We all pay rent and mortgages, eat food, send children
to school. Think in human terms.

Consider these classifications when developing direct mailings to reach and keep in contact with them. In light of their relationship with clients, personalize and customize such mailings. If
you offer them a slew of broad-based, nondescript material, it is
likely to find its way to the round file.

Develop unique and specialized mailings to each professional. Keep up on newspapers and journals in order to pitch specific
ideas that are timely. For example, if there is a real estate topic in
the news recently — perhaps the sale of a large building down-
town, or a lot of activity in one geographic market — show how it
could have been more advantageous to combine it with charitable
vehicles.

Make sure the text and tone suits the particular financial
market. Have it reviewed *before sending* by an appropriate technical committee member (so you do not look stupid in case there is a
glaring error — rebuilding credibility is too costly).

If a different version for different professions (aiming specifically, at how they relate to clients) is too costly for the organization's size, then do *one idea* aimed at *one of the markets*, but send it to
all advisors. Add your own personality to the letter and rotate this
plan among professionals accordingly.

Putting Together a Seminar for Professionals

Seminars, of course, are another device to reach these professionals. Typically an organization sponsors a seminar for financial professionals without giving thought to their needs and wants. They must be treated just as donors are — as a market; you need to know their wants and needs *before* designing the seminar. Even if what you hope to achieve is leveraging rather than gifts. You cannot have a successful seminar without planning from a "consumer orientation" viewpoint (see chapter 4 on marketing). You must also segment your market. What is a good topic for attorneys may bore the life insurance agent to tears.

Seminars for professionals also often miss the mark because the organization does not understand the rigors and demands of the various financial professions. For example, West Coast stock brokers may work from 6:00 A.M. to 2:00 P.M. (give or take a little). When should they be invited to a seminar? Attorneys and CPAs need every "unit of inventory," or billable hour, they can get in a day (see chapter 7). When is a good time for them? Put yourself in their shoes.

Also, you will need to face the truth that many professionals just do not care about charitable giving. Inviting them to a seminar in that frame of mind dooms you to a "No." If you can identify such persons or groups, you and your technical committee have educational and motivational work to do before an invitation is accepted. Or move on to better target groups.

Keep in mind that seminars are for the purpose of educating the professionals so they know when and how to use gift vehicles. They are not for impressing or hyping. The end result should be a more thorough understanding of how to work with a charitable partner in planning and how to use the charitable tools for dynamic results for the client.

An effective way to avoid pitfalls is to generate a simple mission statement for your seminar. I always use this exercise with my seminar clients in order to help focus on exactly what they wish to achieve. Start with these two sentences: "I am having

this seminar because _____. Attendees will go
away from this seminar knowing _____." Complete
these sentences using as few words as possible. This will give you
focus, and everything else will flow from here — the goal, the content, the topics, the audience, etc. Integrate the results of these sentences into your invitation and follow-up calls. Often my client
will say, "Oh, just let me say it in two or three sentences." No, focus, focus, focus. Say it in one compelling, not general or vague,
sentence. It will color and shape the rest of your planning.

In order to reach a particular field, look to your technical
committee for advice. Ask them for lists of memberships in their
fields for mailings and seminars. Try purchasing lists or go directly to the professional associations. They generally sell or give out
their lists. For example, try the local Probate and Trust section, the
Estate Planning Council, the IAFP chapter, the CLU chapter, the
local NASD chapter and real estate associations. They are all out
there; you need to do a little research and maybe a little talking.

Refer to your Chronology and develop a one idea letter. That
means a very short letter with only one idea. Too short to put
down. By the time the addressee figures out whether to keep or
trash this piece of mail, the idea is conveyed. Send it and then follow-up with phone calls or visits. This lays the foundation for
seminars. Go again to your technical committee members regarding the feasibility of a seminar and ask what they would like to
hear and what their colleagues might be interested in. Keep a tally
and ask those committee members to leverage that survey for you
by calling friends and asking the same questions. For example, if
you have thirty people on your technical committee you will tally
results of whether they think a seminar is a good idea and what
topics are of interest. Then, if each of these thirty people calls three
friends you will have multiplied your results to ninety people.
This serves two purposes — it gathers information regarding
what is needed, and it alerts / interests a broader range of partici-
pants.

Tally your results and determine the feasibility of a seminar
at this time; then focus on your topics. When and where should
you hold it — breakfast, lunch, after work, during the day? Be sure
to consider each profession. Should it be held in a financial dis-

trict, at the organization or somewhere else? Will you need a conference room, hotel, restaurant or other meeting room? Once I was asked by a PGO and a consultant to present to professionals for a county hospital. I said I did not believe the proper foundation had been laid. They basically told me to mind my own business. They sent waves of mailings — cold — and got absolutely zero responses. They had to call to cancel my contract. I really wanted to say, "I told you so," but I bit my tongue. I guarantee that foundation surveys and meetings and phone calls will work.

Remember that different information is needed by the different professions relating to their "product" or "services." You need to allay fears that a charitable gift will result in loss of a client or business. This type of talk *must* be focused along the lines of how each profession makes its money. For example, in showing a stock broker how a trust can *enhance* buying and selling opportunities when the market is right because the trust is tax-exempt and no gains are incurred, will help him/her find new prospects or sales.

Professionals will only respond to seminars that will offer them information they can use. Find out what each profession needs. Check out other seminars to find out what they usually do not get. Do not just repeat tired information.

Who should present the seminar? Should there be a single presenter, multiple presenters or a panel presentation? A panel presentation requires the ability to effectively coordinate it, otherwise it is merely multiple presenters. The panel format is the hardest and most time consuming for the staff to coordinate. It is the one that fails most easily and simply becomes seriatim, uncoordinated speakers.

Should it be in lecture form or question and answer form? In either case, keep the discussion specific, focusing on how to use vehicles in *planning*, rather than offering a dissertation on taxes or vehicles, or how to determine the charitable intent of clients.

Be strategic about how much written material will be presented. Again, do not overwhelm them. Use specific outlines, diagrams of gift structures, charts of benefits and computer printouts. It should also be noted that seminars in consortium with other charities save on cost and ease any undue pressure by one organization.

Be sure to follow-up with a letter of thanks to attendees and reiterate your availability to them for help in planned giving.

Personal meetings are an even more effective way to get to know these professionals — if you do not push your luck. It is a good idea to set a time limit on such meetings or you might get carried away while the other person seriously needs to get back to work. Be respectful. Unless you are specifically invited to stay longer, stick to your limit whether you have covered everything or not. Because it is the nature of their services for professionals like these to be "always busy," the old "while-I-have-you-on-the-phone" technique also tends to only irritate them.

Your topic in these one-on-one meetings depends on the advisor, but be sure to show how you can help their client. Describe and explain your role versus theirs in terms of their client's needs. Be confident in your knowledge of these aspects, i.e., make sure you have some knowledge of these aspects because not only is your credibility at stake, but so is their willingness to help.

We all know that memory retention argues against the blitz of organizational information, so tell them one exciting thing — and only one — about your organization instead. Do not just thank them, but tell them to call if they require further information. Let them know you have access to other specialists as well. End your meeting expressing the hope that you can be of service to him / her, and the clients s / he represents. End your meeting on time.

Putting on a Donor Seminar

In reaching through and often beyond these professionals to the donors themselves, the donor seminar is the most popular form of educating the potential gift-maker.

Seminars are a method of communicating an already developed idea. They must, therefore, be extremely well planned, both in the target market and in the topic to be covered. Seminars exist for the purpose of educating the constituency, creating visibility and communicating certain concepts. Are donor seminars de-

signed as a solicitation device, too? What is the expectation of su-
pervisors who approved budget allocation?

The purpose for having a donor seminar must be clearly
identified by the planned giving officer as well as the development director, the executive and the board. Too often, the expectation is that a donor seminar will result in significant gifts. If this is
the purpose of the seminar, direct solicitations would work much
better. This makes the purpose of the seminar an even more crucial starting point.

Because no one (except retirees) really has time to just up and
go to a meeting on the options of planned giving, broad-based
seminars are rarely successful. Eyeing the target market is essential.

The first step in preparing a donor seminar is to check markets within the "community" of the organization (refer to chapter
4 on marketing). Different markets exist, and the means of communicating to those markets will necessarily be different. An effective donor seminar will work with a specific market to
communicate one or more specific ideas especially designed for
that market.

A broad-based seminar might only be warranted if the organization has a small constituency or if particular markets are
small. Perhaps certain smaller market segments could be combined into one donor seminar. An example of a current market for
an organization to hold a seminar for, may be the forty to fifty
year-old professionals who have lost IRA and other pension plan
deductions this year, or simply need to put more away for retirement. That market would not be combined with the retiree market. Those people are already retired and have different concerns
— safe, stable income. The message you want to deliver is entirely
different.

Retirees may be the only group willing and able to find the
time to attend a donor seminar. Others need to be properly motivated by preliminary mailings and contact. Each mailing and contact should contain one exciting idea geared entirely to that
market. It should entice with the idea that further information of
this nature will be presented at this seminar.

In choosing who to invite to such a seminar, determine a

pre-selected gift level or a pre-selected target market. By doing this, you will get your best response rate and highest interest level. Think also about prior donors, board volunteers and close supporters, but be sure to employ the "two-sentence rule" again. Spell out to yourself and others what this seminar is about and what attendees will gain from attending it.

Do not hesitate to reach out to the community in general if your marketing ideas are conducive to a broad-based seminar. Still, researching specific markets is likely to prove more fruitful.

The first step necessary to reaching the market is undertaking a mini feasibility study as to whether a seminar is of interest to or would be effective with a particular market.

Once a determination has been made that such a seminar is feasible, it is necessary to "talk it up" among the board, volunteers and other close supporters. This is for the purpose of getting feedback as to the feasibility of the proposed seminar, as well as to generate interest in attending the seminar. Talking it up has to include motivational topics that will be covered with an enticement that there is more to come.

Direct mail is the most effective technique in reaching possible seminar attendees. The direct mail piece should be absolutely clear as to when, where and what will be presented and who will be presenting. It is amazing how many times such mailings go out without clarifying this information. If a person needs to fight to find out where the seminar will be held, attendance will be low. If access to the location is difficult, a map should be provided. A return card should be provided, which includes space for the attendee to write down any specific topics that the s/he would like to have covered. Postage should be applied to the return card, if possible.

However, do not simply rely on return cards from direct mail, start a phone follow-up campaign to determine if the mail piece was received and if the person is considering attending the seminar. If you feel that one of the volunteers or any committee member may be of help in securing the attendance of a person to whom you have spoken on the phone, jot that down and be sure to call the appropriate volunteer or committee member.

The most interesting place for donors to meet is clearly at the organization, particularly if they can witness part of the program being served on their way to or from the seminar. It will give them a feeling of closeness to the program each time they are invited to the location.

In a series of seminars I presented for a public television station, we tried every meeting place imaginable. The most successful was when we could not find a room and had to hold it in a studio that was not in use that evening. Many people wanted the chance to see the inside workings of the station. It brought them closer to the reality of the operation. Many gifts were closed that night.

A hotel conference room may also be used with great effectiveness, particularly if the hotel is willing to donate the space. Some hotels will give a very nice room with flowers, perhaps coffee, tea, wine, cheese, etc. to a donor group, understanding that it is doing its own marketing at the same time. If you use such a hotel room, be sure to give credit to the hotel for the contribution.

Another option is a host's home. You may ask one of your major supporters, volunteer members or board members to host a donor seminar in his/her home. This is also an effective technique and less formal than either the organization or the hotel. Generally, it is quite clear that the host has been a major supporter in the past. This adds motivation because the host can say a few words about his/her involvement with the organization.

If you have major corporate supporters or a person on the board who is a high-level corporate executive, you may ask that the corporate board room be made available for a donor seminar. Although there are generally fewer catering services in such a board room, the atmosphere is generally one that is fairly elegant or luxurious and provides a nice background.

Mix it up if you can. Use all of the above at different times to retain the interest of donors in continually attending seminars.

Remember, it is absolutely necessary to vary the time of seminars according to the target market selected for the particular seminar. The most successful time slots are: lunch from 12 noon to 2:00 P.M., afternoon from 4:00 to 6:00, early evening from 5:00 or 5:30 to 7:00 or 7:30 and evening from 7:00 until 9:00. The time slot from 7:00 P.M until 9:00 P.M. is clearly more convenient for working

couples; however, it is not conveniet for working couples with
children. The time slot from 5:00 P.M. to 7:00 P.M. may be best if the
seminar is to be held near the place of work, in order to catch people before they leave the work area. Lunch or 4:00 P.M. to 6:00 P.M.
seem to be good times for the retired population.

The rule of thumb is that the seminar should be no longer
than two hours with sufficient breaks, with no more than forty-
five minutes to a maximum of one hour devoted to presentation
between breaks.

In general, the format should follow what is called the "Sandwich" form. There should be an introduction by someone important, such as the board chairman or a major donor, or someone well
known in philanthropy. A community figure could also make the
introduction. The introductory presentation should be no more
than ten minutes long and it should concern either philanthropy in
general or, better yet, it should be focused on this particular organization. It should convey the excitement, the potential, the future or
the accomplishments of this organization. If presented by a community leader, it could refer to this particular organization's role in
the community and the service it has provided.

If presented by someone closer to the organization, it should
involve current topics or issues in the organization or perhaps its
outstanding role among organizations of its type. But no reference
to funds, fund raising or money should be made.

Following the introduction should be a speaker, multiple
speakers or a panel for a presentation of forty-five minutes to one
hour. If longer, breaks are mandatory. Sufficient time should always be given for questions and answers, possibly during the presentation itself. In forty-five minutes, a panel discussion is a little
disjointed. No matter what form of presentation — multiple
speakers or single — written material with the name of the organization on it and the date of the seminar should be handed out to
each participant. Written material regarding the organization in
general should be easily available at the back of the room or on
each seat. Perhaps materials on various gift techniques on cases
could be distributed at the same time.

The close, after the speaker has finished, may be made by a
staff member or volunteer. Again, this portion should be non-

technical or non-fund raising (in a direct, hard-sell sense), and relate to how gift funds support the wonderful things happening at
the organization at this point. In addition, an invitation should be
extended to donors to use some particular service of the organization. Keep in mind that donors become donors when they have
developed a strong linkage to the organization.

Use of the organization's services, if possible, is the best way
to get the donor closer. For example, a university where I spoke invited a close-by retirement community to a university building for
a donor seminar. The seminar topic was financial and estate planning in general. The president of the university made a spectacu-
lar ten minute presentation regarding the role of that university,
both in the community and nationwide, and he discussed what
fields it excelled in and how it ranked in various other fields. The
president also suggested that donors should feel free to come on
campus at any time and to attend any classes — to sit in as they
wished. For free. The audience was genuinely excited and pleased
with the offer. They talked about it for some time after the seminar.

After the close by a staff member or an official of the organization, a social hour may follow for somewhere between thirty
and forty-five minutes. Appropriate refreshments should be provided. The speaker(s) should remain available during this time
for specific questions. The speaker should be prepped to note who
asks specific questions regarding charitable gifts in order to discuss them later with the planned giving officer. The volunteer
committee definitely should be present to greet and socialize.
Technical committee members and marketing committee members may be asked to attend as well, in order to be available for
questions.

Follow-up to a seminar is absolutely essential. Phone calls
and letters should thank the person for his/her attendance and
should ask whether they have any questions regarding any of the
topics.

The organization may wish to consider offering the services
of volunteer technical advisors to answer these questions, after
the technical advisors approve the donation of their time. The organization may also consider offering the services of an attorney
or consultant who is paid by the organization to consult with spe-

cific donors (prospects) if they are interested in structuring or discussing a potential charitable gift.

In choosing speakers for a donor seminar, be advised, or perhaps warned, that good technical skills do not equal good speaking skills. Have personal talks with potential speakers and note the following:

- articulation
- tone of voice
- grammar
- timid/aggressive approach
- colorful analogies and examples
- explanation of technicalities
- enthusiasm
- gestures

If it is at all possible, the best method of evaluating a speaker is to go someplace to listen to a speech. Get recommendations from others in the community, particularly from your technical advisory or marketing committees.

Be careful to invite the speaker "properly." For example, if it is the top estate planner in your community, perhaps the executive, president, or chairman of the board should do the inviting. Be sensitive to standing and rank in the community. Also, be sensitive to how such standing and rank may affect audience feeling.

When inviting the speaker or speakers, be frank regarding your need to mutually set the topic and tone of the presentation. And, of course, pay them because you need to set the rules. If you expect services for free, the service provider will seek other forms of compensation, such as how many clients s/he may pick up. It is far better to pay for services and be in control of the seminar, the topic and the contact. After all, these are your prospects and your donors and you have certain needs in that regard. You need to keep the organization in the forefront, not the advisor. This must be understood up front. Examples of advisors forgetting this are too numerous to count. The advisor often takes over and markets his/her own services, to the dismay of the organization. If the advisor breaches this agreement, obviously s/he should never be invited back.

A related question concerns how much the speaker should refer to the charitable organization in examples regarding estate planning and charitable giving. It is a delicate balance to be decided by each organization. Particularly, you do not want to bludgeon the audience with too many references to charitable giving to the hosting organization. They already know why they are there.

Specific topics must be chosen for better results once target markets have been selected. Consider having topic-specific donor seminars instead of a shotgun approach. For example:

- Wills clinic
- Estate planning for the younger crowd
- Estate planning for real estate holdings
- Estate planning for unmarried people
- Estate planning for married couples with two families
- Helping your children/grandchildren
- Planning for retirement
- Estate planning after retirement
- Dynamic charitable giving techniques for the affluent
- Year-end tax planning

These seminars are not just meant to be informational, but persuasive. Your format and your presenter should show these donors how they can make a planned gift work for them. That is your job, is it not?

7

Use of Consultants and Attorneys in Planned Giving

Russell Sage, financier, whose wife set up the Russell Sage Foundation (1907):

Sage's lawyer was delighted by the case his client had just laid before him. 'It's an ironclad case,' he exclaimed with confidence. 'We can't possibly lose!'

'Then we won't sue,' said Sage. 'That was my opponent's side of the case I gave you.'

— The Little Brown Book of Anecdotes

Consultants and attorneys play a prominent role in the "process" of planned giving. If dealt with properly, they both can be instrumental in the success of your program. If not, well, you guessed it.

If you are interested in getting help from a planned giving consultant, you have already proven smart enough to identify some of your program's weaknesses. It is not always as easy to find weaknesses as strengths. Sit down and examine those weaknesses before making any other moves. Where is it that you need help? Write it down in detail. Be honest.

Then, in looking to a consultant who can help, try to match your

weaknesses with their strengths. There are consultants who specialize in different aspects of the "process," so you must find out
who can best meet your needs. This may challenge your interviewing skills. Remember, however, that consultants first need to learn
as much about your program as you do about them. They have to be
more than a hired gun.

There are primarily seven different types of planned giving
consultants. One type handles donor visits and solicitations. This
consultant will participate in your program almost as an extended
staff member to help you with specifically identified donor visits
for the purpose of cultivation or solicitation. This person can be a
beneficial extension to your current ability to carry on a planned
giving program. Quite often this consultant works with smaller
organizations where there is either an executive director or a development director performing all the functions, but no planned
giving staff member.

Another type of consultant performs evaluations of donor
records and determines the feasibility of the program. This type of
consultant often works on a project basis as opposed to having an
ongoing consulting relationship. This service may also be combined with other forms of consulting done on an ongoing basis.
The purpose of using this consultant is to get a reading on whether
the organization's donor history would support the beginnings of
a planned giving program.

Some consultants have a hand in all duties — essentially sub-
stituting for staff. Some smaller organizations wishing to undertake planned giving cannot afford to hire a full-time staff person.
These consultants work for those organizations one or two days
per week on an independent contractor status and generally act as
a planned giving staff person.

Others strictly handle technical support, and tax and legal issues. Some consultants who are not attorneys or CPAs are nevertheless quite competent in the area of providing technical support
for a program. This might include writing or reviewing brochures
and newsletters, and becoming involved with the organization in
its gift structuring for prospects.

Not enough planned giving programs take advantage of
consultants offering marketing support. This type can perform

marketing studies and help to identify target markets. The consultant may help expand markets beyond those which the organization thought existed. S/he can also help design more effective methods of communications to reach those markets.

Another type of consultant deals with setting up the internal structure, management and funds administration. This consultant reviews the internal structure for its strengths, weaknesses, needs for coordination and readiness to undertake a planned giving program. S/he creates the program's infrastructure. This consultant is absolutely necessary at the initial stages of planned giving or when reviving a planned giving program. Early coordination among the various offices, particularly funds administration, is crucial to laying a good foundation for planned giving.

Board development consultants who are working to strengthen nonprofit boards are not only known to planned giving consultants, but to development offices and nonprofit organizations in general. If there are extreme problems with the strength of the board or filling vacancies, this type of consultant can be very helpful.

Check the qualifications of consultants before taking them on. Get referrals from other organizations or discover their general reputations by contacting industry groups such as NSFRE, NAHD, CASE, NCPG and AAM. Find out about their experience in the field and talk to former or current fund-raising staff. Be attuned to the possibility of problems that may occur when transferring skills or if, for example, a planned giving staff member of an ongoing program becomes a consultant and has never created a planned gift program. A successful program at another organization does not necessarily make one a good consultant, particularly if the planned giving staff person came into an ongoing program or one that differs from their past experience. For example, a person with staff experience entirely at a college or university with a developed program may have no idea at all how to set up a new program for an environmental organization. At the same time, there may also be advantages to a consultant with current, hands-on experience.

Before choosing, again identify your needs. It is absolutely essential for the organization to consider why it needs a consultant, which of the roles listed above it may perform and which roles it must have outside counsel perform.

Organizations typically understand that they need to interview and interrogate a consultant with whom they may have a long relationship. In the interview process, it is important to determine whether the person in question (or the person to be assigned) is technically competent in relation to the field of services s/he provides. His/her experience should include both breadth (numbers and different types of organizations) and depth (long-term association either on staff or in a consulting role) in order to understand the true problems of that field. In the interview process the organization should also explore the consultant's feeling about his/her own work. Another topic to discuss is the consultant's view of projected trends in his/her field.

The consultant should be able to furnish the organization with clear information, both oral and written, on results accomplished in other organizations. Keep in mind that some information may be confidential; nevertheless, enough should be public so that one can tell whether the person has achieved his/her stated objectives.

A series of "what if" questions should be posed to the consultant in the interview as well. The "what if" questions should revolve around the nature of the duties of that particular consultant. For example, a marketing consultant might be asked, "What if the organization has a small group of loyal supporters, but has been unable to extend that group out into the community? How could we begin to translate that close-in support to a more expanded marketplace?" An example for a consultant engaging in a study of the internal structure in funds administration might be, "What if funds administration has handled nothing but cash and securities to date? How do we go about beginning to get funds administration to coordinate with the development office in a planned giving effort?" The "what ifs" should turn up specific information, not that you are asking for free advice during the interview stage, but you are checking to see if the person understands the question and has enough knowledge to formulate a good answer.

An off-the-cuff assessment of what you should do in general may be useful. Ask the consultant to give you an initial reading of where you stand with regard to your planned giving program and let him/her do the talking.

Who should participate in the interview? The executive director, the director of development, the planned giving officer and probably at least one person from the board who will be closely involved with planned giving should participate.

Remember to request three references and then follow-up on them. Make sure you are comfortable with what the referring parties say. Ask the three referring parties to give you names of other organizations that they might know have used the same consultant. Then check on these references not given by the consultant. If you feel comfortable with the references the consultant gave and those you found on your own, you probably have a good choice.

Check whether the consultant has repeat or ongoing clients. This generally indicates satisfaction over the long term with the consultant's work and results. During the process of choosing a consultant, the explanation of why you need a consultant should be perfectly clear. In discussions, the consultant's explanation should also be perfectly clear as to why s/he feels his/her consulting services specifically meet those stated needs.

Then, put it in writing. In order to make it clear that both you and the consultant understand what is expected of him/her, write up a contract that explains in detail the duties to be performed. This is a meeting of the minds that should be made as a formal agreement, clearly stating the types of services to be provided. The term of the contract should also be clearly stated and any renewal periods or options should be set forth in the agreement. The price of the contract should be negotiated and decided on from the beginning, and the fee for consulting should also be established.

Consulting fees range widely, and in planned giving the difference often rests upon the fact that many people engaged in planned giving consulting are at the same time on staff at another organization, where they have arranged to have one or two days off per month. This type of consultant does not need to carry an overhead and is generally less expensive. The established consultant or consulting firm generally working full-time for the business must operate out of an office with overhead. This consultant will be more expensive, but will generally have more time to devote to your project. There also will be fewer conflicts of interest.

It should be made clear up front what costs will be charged through to the nonprofit client and what items are expected to be reimbursed. When you are expected to pay the consulting fee is an important item to be discussed at the time the contract is made.

If the contract is in written form, does it lock the organization into a twelve-month, twenty-four month or thirty-six month period without ability to break the contract? The organization should attempt to secure a provision for either evaluation and termination or simply termination if it is not satisfied. That is why it is important to clearly state what is to be accomplished in a written contract, or if it is discussed it should be written in note form or in a follow-up letter.

In the choosing, interviewing and contract formation stages, you should also discuss with the consultant methods for evaluating his/her work. You should agree upon a method from the beginning. Write out your objectives to be accomplished on a timeline, just as in the chronology in chapter 2, and use those same objectives as evaluation measuring devices.

Understand that those objectives are guidelines for what should be achieved on a projected timeline. Time lags may occur that are not in the control of the consultant, and certain things may not be accomplished which may not be the fault of the consultant, but rather internal or external problems in the organization. Nevertheless, setting a time-frame with objectives will also set your evaluation techniques.

Consultants generally do not bill for time spent in the proposal stages with a nonprofit organization when they are determining if there is a match-up of knowledge and need. However, if the proposal time turns into transferral of actual knowledge, the organization is often billed by the consultant. Generally, consultants will bill on a daily basis, $250 to $6,000 per day, or perhaps they will have a monthly retainer fee. Some consultants who engage in work based on a twelve, twenty-four or thirty-six month period will give an annual fee for their work. Be aware that fees charged on a daily, monthly or yearly basis must include and cover the non-paid proposal time spent on your organization and others. If this were not the case consultants could not remain in business.

Let us now turn to the use of attorneys in the planned giving program, and which type of attorney should be used, and when.

There are basically four different types of attorneys: staff attorney, outside counsel, attorney on board and pro bono attorney.

The selection among the above four will depend upon the size of the organization and the budget. In all events, an organization should pay for its legal advice. Whether or not an organization can afford to have a person on staff who is knowledgeable about charitable giving is a matter only the organization will know the answer to. However, the organization should not use a staff attorney who is not knowledgeable in charitable giving, unless that attorney is willing to undertake a couple of years of study to learn the ins and outs of a new field.

Not many attorneys are versed, in-depth, on charitable vehicles, or how to plan for them. If they do have knowledge of charitable vehicles, quite often they are familiar only with the donor's side, which is understandable if that is who they regularly represent. However, if they tend to not be sensitive to the donee's side, they may never pursue the other opportunities planned giving offers to donors.

We will talk about using an outside attorney a little later, but first let us consider an attorney who is on the board. Keep in mind that the primary role of the person involved is that of board member, not an attorney. In fact, there may be an inherent conflict of interest, where the board member in his/her role as director would desire one result, but as an attorney must give another opinion. Also, deriving substantial economic benefit while on the board may be a conflict of interest.

Unfortunately, on many nonprofit boards, attorneys dominate and insist that their firm receive the work from the organization. Some state Attorneys General look disfavorably at such practices As to a pro bono volunteer or the board member taking the work into his/her firm to do it voluntarily, understand that the volunteer or board member, generally a senior level person, will rarely touch the work. It will be assigned to a lower level associate, who has disposable time (or so the partner believes), but the lower level associate has a high billable hour requirement per month. Thus, the work will be pushed back and pushed back in lieu of billing hours necessary

to advance him/her in the firm. In some cases, the lower level associate will become involved with the organization and actually enjoy
the work. This case, however, is rare. Generally, it is just another ob-
ligation of the job.

What services should be offered by an attorney delivering
services to the planned giving market? Basically, the drafting of
documents, obtaining of private letter rulings where necessary,
planning gift structures, planning the overall estate for a donor in
some instances, meeting with donors and with advisors, making
presentations and training inside and outside persons involved
with the organization, alerting the nonprofit as to pitfalls and
traps in proposed gifts, providing legal and tax updates, protecting the nonprofit and avoiding exposure to risk and law suits,
helping to establish guidelines and policies (e.g. undue influence,
ethics, unauthorized practice of law) and preparing or presenting
seminars for donors.

You will face a variety of experiences concerning the need for
outside counsel. In a planned giving program that has existed for
a while you will come across all types of proposed assets, vehicles
and structures. After a while you will begin to think that none of
the things that you see will ever occur again. (And maybe you
hope that is true.) The lawyer can help in these areas because s/he
will have knowledge, either by him/herself or along with others
in the firm, as to:

- real estate
- corporate law
- securities
- contracts
- estates and trusts
- exempt organization problems
- unrelated business income
- state laws regarding solicitation
- endowments
- probate

It is only human nature that when you work with a donor
you will want to receive the gift. It is essential for you to have gift

structures reviewed by outside counsel for their objectivity as to whether this gift is appropriate for the donee and for the donor. Simply said, you need a second check, an independent judgement.

The attorney you select should have or should be able to develop the ability to work with reluctant advisors to try to persuade them to understand the charitable intent of the donor and the structure proposed. You can use your attorney as an "expert" that you offer to other advisors because you are aware that this is an area of technical specialty.

In many situations, you may use your attorney as a buffer or a shield by using the respect and credibility of the legal profession to advance positions that you take or to obtain things that you need.

Be aware that the level of experience in charitable giving is the most critical factor in working with your outside attorney. There are two different types of attorneys who may say that they know "charitable giving:" one knows it from the donor's point of view, understanding vehicles and structures from an estate planning perspective, while the other knows it from the nonprofit point of view, understanding the donor/donee relationship and the needs and functions of the nonprofit organization.

In some areas it is difficult to find a knowledgeable attorney. You may need to train your lawyer in charitable giving. If that is the case, how may lawyers be classified and which may be best suited to your needs? Examine six different types of lawyers and their expertise in charitable giving:

(1) The fund-raising attorney. Certain attorneys specialize in working with fund raisers and have knowledge of both fund-raising techniques and legal questions that arise during the fund-raising process, as well as funds administration, exempt organization matters and related questions. It is especially helpful if this attorney has had staff experience either as in-house legal counsel or directly in fund raising.

(2) Exempt organization lawyer. This lawyer often has knowledge both in exempt organization legal and status matters as well as in charitable giving. This lawyer can be very helpful to your program but, of course, is almost as difficult to find as the

fund-raising attorney.

(3) The tax lawyer or estate planner. Many tax lawyers and estate planners have some degree of knowledge of charitable vehicles. Some of them even have a great deal of knowledge of charitable vehicles; however, that does not mean that they understand the donor/donee relationship or the needs of the nonprofit itself. These persons are advocates or representatives of the individual client. Nevertheless, this type of lawyer may be very knowledgeable in gift structures. The structures will no doubt be for the benefit of the individual client as opposed to the best structure for the donee. You will need to retrain them to think "donee." And, of course, the bulk of lawyers in this area have no knowledge of charitable giving at all and do not seem to care to learn it.

(4) The business lawyer. Although the business lawyer will not have a great knowledge of charitable giving, if this is the only lawyer available to you, it may be well worth your while to undertake training him/her. A business lawyer, if a good one, generally tries to work out creative solutions and help his/her client make things happen. That quality is invaluable in a charitable giving attorney as well.

(5) General large law firm. The large law firm may or may not have a charitable giving specialist, but the number of law firms with a charitable giving specialist is small. Therefore, you are almost always choosing a large firm with expertise in various traditional areas of law. What happens when charitable giving questions arise? Generally, these are assigned to someone the partner feels either has time to learn it (for which you pay dearly) or whose area is most closely aligned (but not exactly) with the question asked. The one major problem with dealing with large law firms is that there are many levels of review and many hours that are put into a problem or question, resulting in enormous billing by some firms. An example is the $100,000 charged by an East Coast law firm for the creation of a pooled income fund.

One advantage of a large law firm is that there are many attorneys with expertise in different areas, so that when unusual questions come up regarding securities, contracts, patents, real estate or the like, there will be someone in the law firm who can respond to those questions. You need to weigh the advantages and disadvantages of the general large law firm. Interview them well to find out who *really* knows charitable giving, if anyone.

(6) Purchase of a name. Quite often nonprofit boards are impressed with "big name" law firms and want to attach the name of one of these law firms to a specific project, thereby giving the impression of its blessing. This is almost always disastrous and very costly to you. For the most part, the law firm does not have expertise in charitable giving and will spend a lot of time and money researching your project. You will get a very legal-like (legalese) memo. You would have been much better off using any of the lawyers in any of the other categories in the list above.

In finding the right type of lawyer who meets your needs, use referrals from other nonprofit organizations as aggressively as possible, calling at least ten or twelve organizations to get referrals.

Call law school estate planning professors. Having read many articles or attended speeches, these people generally know who is knowledgeable in the field of charitable giving relating to estate planning.

Contact your local bar association trust section and the estate planning council in your area. Generally, if an attorney specializes in charitable giving, it will be known to members of those groups.

Look in journals and newsletters for articles on charitable giving written by lawyers. Read those articles, do not simply assume that the attorney knows what s/he is talking about. Read them for technical correctness. If you do not have technical expertise, at least read them for common sense. If the person sounds like somebody to your liking, call the person. It is easy to find individual members through telephone information. The city is almost always given in an article.

Ask staff attorneys who work for nonprofits, even if those staff attorneys do not work in the charitable giving area, for the names of charitable giving lawyers. Quite often they are familiar with attorneys or rely on attorneys in charitable giving.

Once you have located a few attorneys of interest to you, begin the selection process. Interview your attorney aggressively. It is interesting, and puzzling, to note how many people do not think about interviewing attorneys. Attorneys are, however, your employees; they work *for* you, therefore, they should be interviewed just as a consultant or another employee would be interviewed.

It is also important for you to develop a "case study" which you can use with the attorney in the interview. This should be a particular gift situation that you have faced where you needed legal help. Check to see if the lawyer has any response at all to this and if the response sounds reasonable. Also explore the attorney's feelings regarding philanthropy in general.

Ask the attorney whether s/he has participated in any philanthropic endeavors or has volunteered for any organizations. Explore whether there is an understanding of the "heart" of the nonprofit. For example, how it really works. If the attorney exhibits no understanding or no desire to understand, there should be no job offered.

Avoid "The Big Deal Prevention Department." Many lawyers simply like to tear down what others suggest without offering creative solutions for circumventing problems. Avoid this attorney like the plague. You need a partner in fund raising who can, nevertheless, be objective and keep you out of trouble.

Check their "adversary quotient" as well. You will need cooperation not battles or ego problems or other stress and tension between you and the attorney. You do not need to be told that you are wrong or to be given the impression that you do not have any knowledge. Get someone pleasant.

The greatest area of misunderstanding among nonprofit organizations is attorneys' fees. It is an area you should discuss freely and openly with your attorney at the beginning of the relationship and at any time that you see problems cropping up.

Generally, attorneys bill on an hourly basis, but sometimes they will bill on a retainer, generally a monthly amount. There are rarely contracts that are signed for any set number of months.

The concept of "billable time" is broken down into inventory of time units. Every attorney has an inventory of time which s/he holds out to the public for sale. This is the equivalent of the inventory in a product business. These units must be sold in order to bring gross revenue to the firm. The firm then needs to pay all of its expenses to come up with a profit margin. What the attorney has to offer to clients, then, is his/her time. Therefore, time spent on one client (and away from other clients) must be billed.

The units must be sold by each attorney. For example, assume that there are ten lawyers in a firm and each has a usable seven-hour day. This means that the law firm has seventy units that it may sell to the public times five days a week for a total of 350 units of inventory available a week.

If too many of these units are given away in a week, there will be no more law business because it will not be able to cover its costs. It is unfair for client after client to ask the attorney to give free time. Consider for a moment that the 350 units referred to above are equivalent to pairs of shoes in a shoe store. How many of those 350 pairs could be given away during the week and the store still be able to stay in business? There will be a point at which the shoe store cannot cover its costs.

Unfortunately, some people in nonprofit organizations do not understand this concept and view themselves as the only ones asking for a "free pair of shoes." They cannot understand why they should be billed. But, when the law firm is asked to give away many pairs of shoes per week, it should be understandable that the lawyer simply cannot comply with the request. Therefore, be considerate of the attorney's time and realize that time is his/her only inventory and that s/he needs to sell it.

Keep in mind that the attorney does not "make" what s/he "bills." If an hourly rate of $125 or $150 is quoted to you, that does not mean the attorney takes it home.

Lawyers are the profit centers, personally. All of the staff are "cost" items, plus there are other expenses including office, library, insurance, etc., that represent costs. The lawyer's sale of time must cover everything else in the firm. All of this is equally applicable to CPAs.

Some nonprofit planned giving officers have never worked with professionals who bill by the hour. If you find yourself in this situation, based on what is described in this section, have an open and frank discussion with your attorney about billing — or this could be your worst nightmare (the open-ended bill). Learn what is and what is not billable, so you have no unpleasant surprises when the bill comes. Make sure that the attorney bills regularly.

If you follow this advice, your working relationship with your consultant and your attorney will be a pleasant and happy experience.

8

Ethics, Undue Influence, Conflicts of Interest and Fiduciary Responsibility

A man can stand a lot as long as he can stand himself.
— Alex Munthe, *Remarks of Famous People*

A system of moral principles: rules of conduct recognized by a particular group or culture; a set of values relating to human conduct with respect to rightness and wrongness of actions; rules or standards for right conduct or practice of a profession. That is a pretty thorough definition of ethics, right from your dictionary.

The lack of stated, specific ethical rules regarding planned giving suggests this is a crucial definition involved in the "process" to keep in mind. It is the nature of the beast that issues of ethics pop up time and time again in planned giving, so be prepared.

Planned giving, and development overall, has struggled to identify itself as a "profession." So have other disciplines, such as CPAs, CLUs and CFPs. The CPA designation is now well accepted as a professional designation, although it was not long ago that they had to exert their efforts in that direction. CLUs are even more recently recognized as "professionals," and, clearly, CFPs are still fighting an uphill battle. As each "profession" gains its status, it also creates rules of conduct.

Planned giving, or development, has not yet attained the status of "profession" in our society, nevertheless, standards of conduct are needed because of the representation of "donors" and even more so because of the dual nature of that representation.

A planned giving officer has a unique position in relation to both the organization by which s/he is employed and the prospect for whom s/he is planning. The role requires that both parties be adequately represented and protected at the same time. This presents an inherent conflict of interest with consequent uncertainty as to the "right" course of action to be followed, even more evidence for the institution of standards.

Develop ethical guidelines for your planned giving office as soon as possible. Certain basic standards may be borrowed from other professions, such as CPAs and lawyers. But there are other specific points to consider in drafting your statement of ethics. The following guideline models were excerpted from Model Rules of Professional Conduct adopted by the House of Delegates of the American Bar Association and altered as necessary for planned giving.

Responsibilities. There is great responsibility in representation. In all professional functions, a planned giving officer ("PGO") should be competent, prompt and diligent. A PGO's conduct should conform to the requirements of the law and be guided by personal conscience and the approbation of professional peers. S/he should strive to attain the highest level of skill. A PGO's ethical problems arising from conflicts between his/her representations to *donors* and an employing entity should be resolved through the exercise of sensitive and professional moral judgment. It is the rule of reason that ultimately rules.

Who is the *donor* for a PGO? A PGO presents to the charity the prospective donor's intent and represents to the donor the harity's needs. *Both* are "represented" in some sense by the PGO, who represents demand competence.

Competence. Competent handling of a particular donor matter includes inquiry into and analysis of the factual elements of the problem and the use of methods and procedures that meet the standards of competent PGOs in this field. It also includes adequate preparation.

Criminal, fraudulent or sham transactions. A PGO is required to give an honest opinion about the actual consequences that are likely to result from a donor's gift. When the donor's course of action has already begun and is continuing, the PGO's responsibility is especially delicate. A PGO should not participate in a sham transaction. For example, a transaction that may have criminal penalties or include fraudulent escape of tax liability. For this reason, the PGO cannot promise to hold gifted property for two years so no Form 8282 reporting the sale price need be made. That is tax fraud. I am personally aware of one development officer under criminal tax investigation (a very serious matter) for this very representation.

Diligence. A PGO shall act with reasonable diligence and promptness in representing a donor. A PGO should act with commitment and dedication to the interests of the donor. No professional shortcoming is more widely resented than procrastination, and the donor's interests can often be adversely affected by the passage of time or the change of conditions. In extreme circumstances, unreasonable delay can cause a donor needless anxiety and undermine confidence in the PGO's trustworthiness. A PGO should carry through to conclusion all matters undertaken for a donor.

Communication. This is also an important and sometimes delicate issue. A PGO shall keep a donor reasonably informed about the status of a gift transaction and promptly comply with reasonable requests for information. A PGO shall explain a matter to the extent reasonably necessary to permit the donor to make informed decisions, referring the donor to an advisor for explanation of legal and tax consequences. The donor should have sufficient information to participate intelligently in decisions concerning the objectives of the proposed gift and the means by which they are to be pursued. Adequacy of communication depends in part on the kind of outside professional advice or assistance involved.

Confidentiality. A PGO shall not reveal information relating to the representation of a donor. The confidentiality rule applies to all information relating to the gift.

Conflict of interest. A PGO shall not work with a donor if such work will be directly adverse to another donor. The PGO's own interests should not be permitted to have an adverse effect.

Prohibited transactions. A PGO shall not enter into a business transaction with a donor or knowingly acquire an ownership, possessory, security or other pecuniary interest adverse to a donor. A PGO shall not use information relating to a gift to the disadvantage of the donor. S/he shall not provide financial assistance to a donor. S/he shall not accept gifts or loans from the donor.

Charitable entity. The organization employing the PGO is a legal entity, but it cannot act except through its officers, directors, employees, shareholders and other constituents. Duties and responsibilities of the PGO flow to the legal entity through such persons.

Clear justification should exist for seeking review over the head of the person to whom the PGO is responsible. In extreme cases, it may be reasonably necessary for the PGO to refer the matter to the organization's highest authority.

Declining or terminating work with donor. A PGO shall not work with a donor or, where such work has commenced, shall withdraw from such work if (1) the representation will result in a violation of the rules of ethics set forth by NCPG or in violation of a law, (2) the PGO's physical or mental condition materially impairs the PGO's ability to work with the donor or (3) the PGO is discharged.

Giving advice. In working with the donor, the PGO shall exercise independent judgment and give candid advice. In rendering such advice, a PGO may refer to law and tax, and to other considerations such as moral, economic, social and political factors that may be relevant to the donor's situation. However, the PGO may not give legal or tax advice.

Maintaining the integrity of the planned giving profession. A PGO shall not knowingly make a false statement of material fact, or fail to disclose a fact necessary to correct a misunderstanding known by the person to have arisen in the matter, or knowingly fail to respond to a demand for information.

Misconduct. It is misconduct for a PGO to (1) violate or attempt to violate the rules of ethical conduct, knowingly assist or induce another to do so or do so through the acts of another; (2) commit a criminal act that reflects adversely on the PGO's honesty, trustworthiness or fitness as a PGO in other respects; (3) engage in conduct involving dishonesty, fraud, deceit or misrepresentation; (4) engage in conduct that is prejudicial to the administration of justice or (5) state or imply an ability to improperly influence a government agency or other official.

Below is the National Committee on Planned Giving's (NCPG) model standards for conduct, referred to above.

Model Standards of Practice for The Charitable Gift Planner

Preamble

The purpose of this statement is to encourage responsible charitable gift planning by urging the adoption of the following Standards of Practice by all who work in the charitable gift planning process, including the charitable institutions and their gift planning officers, independent fund-raising consultants, attorneys, accountants, financial planners and life insurance agents, collectively referred to hereafter as "Gift Planners."

This statement recognizes that the solicitation, planning and administration of a charitable gift is a complex process involving philanthropic, personal, financial and tax considerations, and, as such, often involves professionals from various disciplines whose goals should include working together to structure a gift that achieves a fair and proper balance between the interests of the donor and the purposes of the charitable institution.

I. Primacy of Philanthropic Motivation

The principal basis for making a charitable gift should be a desire on the part of the donor to support the work of charitable institutions.

II. Explanation of Tax Implications

Congress has provided tax incentives for charitable giving, and the emphasis in this statement on philanthropic motivation in no way minimizes the necessity and appropriateness of a full and accurate explanation by the Gift Planner of those incentives and their implications.

III. Full Disclosure

It is essential to the gift planning process that the role and relationship of all parties involved, including how and by whom each is compensated, be fully disclosed to the donor. A Gift Planner shall not act or purport to act as a representative of any charity without the express knowledge and approval of the charity, and shall not, while employed by the charity, act or purport to act as a representative of the donor, without the express consent of both the charity and the donor.

IV. Compensation

Compensation paid to Gift Planners shall be reasonable and proportionate to the services provided. Payments of finder's fees, commissions or other fees by a donee organization to an independent Gift Planner as a condition for the delivery of a gift are never appropriate. Such payments lead to abusive practices and may violate certain federal and state regulations. Likewise, commission-based compensation for Gift Planners who are employed by a charitable institution is never appropriate.

V. Competence and Professionalism

The Gift Planner should strive to achieve and maintain a high degree of competence in his or her chosen area, and shall advise donors only in areas in which s/he is professionally qualified. It is a hallmark of professionalism for Gift Planners that they realize when they have reached the limits of their knowledge and expertise and, as a result, should include other professionals in the process. Such relationships should be characterized by courtesy, tact and mutual respect.

VI. Consultation with Independent Advisors

A Gift Planner acting on behalf of a charity shall in all cases strongly encourage the donor to discuss the proposed gift with competent independent legal and tax advisors of the donor's choice.

VII. Consultation with Charities

Although Gift Planners frequently and properly counsel donors concerning specific charitable gifts without the prior knowledge or approval of the donee organization, the Gift Planner, in order to ensure that the gift will accomplish the donor's objectives, should encourage the donor, early in the gift planning process, to discuss the proposed gift with the charity to whom the gift is to be made. In cases where the donor desires anonymity, the Gift Planner shall endeavor, on behalf of the undisclosed donor, to obtain the charity's input in the gift planning process.

VIII. Explanation of Gift

The Gift Planner shall make every effort, insofar as it is possible, to ensure that the donor receives a full and accurate explanation of all aspects of the proposed charitable gift.

IX. Full Compliance

A Gift Planner shall fully comply with and shall encourage other parties in the gift planning process to fully comply with both the letter and spirit of all applicable federal and state laws and regulations.

X. Public Trust

Gift Planners shall, in all dealings with donors, institutions and other professionals, act with fairness, honesty, integrity and openness. Except for compensation received for services, the terms of which have been disclosed to the donor, they shall have no vested interest that could result in personal gain.

Adopted and subscribed to by the NATIONAL COMMITTEE ON PLANNED GIVING, representing fifty planned giving councils comprised of 4,000 individuals and involved in planned giving throughout the country, and the COMMITTEE ON GIFT ANNUITIES, representing over 1,200 public charities across America.

It should be said that conflicts of interest come in many shapes and sizes and are not always immediately recognizable. The planned giving officer should make a good faith attempt to recognize when his/her dual "representation" is adverse to either the prospect, because s/he is protecting the entity, or to the entity, because s/he believes s/he is protecting the prospect. The nature of dual representation should call into play extra diligence on the part of the planned giving officer.

An inherent conflict of interest may arise, however, when the planned giving officer needs to meet certain stated quotas and the gift is doubtful. The planned giving officer's interest in the matter *must* be subordinated to the best interests of the prospect.

On the other hand, a reverse conflict of interest may arise when the planned giving officer needs to meet a quota and is uncertain whether the proposed structure is beneficial or detrimental to the organization, such as when the organization is committed by the officer to holding property for a stated period of time for the benefit of the donor (related use, valuation, donee reporting). The planned giving officer must maintain his/her protection of the represented entity over his/her desire to meet personal goals or quotas.

Although a planned giving officer is generally urged to cultivate and befriend donors (prospects), the officer must avoid even the appearance of impropriety, such as cultivating his/her own benefits under a will or trust.

Undue influence must also be addressed in your guidelines. With the advent of an aging generation, nonprofits are more frequently faced with elderly constituents needing assistance — personal and monetary. Often these constituents are widowed, have no children, have children who are well-taken care of or children who live a great distance from them. They are generally in their eighties and nineties or more. It has recently been estimated that 2.2 million people are over the age of eighty-five in this country.

In increasing numbers, this generation is turning to nonprofits for care and help of all types. Quite often the exchange offered is the family home, the residue of the estate or a substantial bequest. The older generation is often abandoned by the younger generations — mostly nieces, nephews, estranged children and grandchildren and distant relatives — who are then appalled to learn that substantial portions of wealth are committed to charity.

Whether or not they should be so surprised, their feelings are often vented in a courtroom once they have filed a suit charging

undue influence against both the member of the organization who
had a close relationship with the deceased, and the organization
itself. Generally, the relief requested is the return of the bequest
and sometimes the return of prior lifetime gifts.

Although certain cases are egregious, many others fall into
the gray zone. Keep in mind that anyone can sue and that defense
is expensive and obligatory to save a gift and avoid a default judgment. That is another important reason why appropriate organizational (a policy matter) and personal (a personal matter) standards
of conduct must be adopted. Organizational policies MUST BE
WRITTEN AND ADHERED TO.

Let us look at three standard-setting cases that better illus-
trate this point:

(1) **Whitmire vs. Kroelinger,** 42 F.2d 699 (W.D. S.C. 1930).
Miss Whitmire died in May 1928. She was born in the town of
Greenville, South Carolina and had a brother to whom she was devoted. Her brother bequeathed to her a great deal of real estate
which, at his death, was of little value. However, after his death, it
grew to be very valuable.

Miss Whitmire, having been his sole heir-at-law, took great
interest in learning about the property. She was considered to
have had good common sense and a streak of firmness or obstina-
cy. She refused to let a single piece of property get away from her.
This was described by the court as "the situation of a maiden lady
sheltered under the old regime of the south, living on for years after the 'old order' had passed away."

When Miss Whitmire died in 1928 her heirs discovered a will
signed in 1923, which they brought suit to set aside for lack of capacity and for undue influence. The claim was that the defendant,
Mr. Kroelinger and the trustees of the Clearwater Baptist Church
in Florida, unduly influenced poor Miss Whitmire and caused her
to transfer substantial pieces of her real estate to the church. The
last will, however, was very similar to two wills which she had
made previously and was a very logical and natural will for her to
have made.

Over the years, from about 1915 to 1923, Miss Whitmire became quite involved with the Clearwater Baptist Church and with

the Reverend. Over time, she became impressed by Mr. Kroelinger and by Mr. Kroelinger's visions of building a brand new church. The town of Clearwater was host to several other religious denominations, and the Baptists were in the distinct minority. She felt a certain urge to help them out of that situation. Mr. Kroelinger had gone along with this urge and, in fact, had encouraged it because he could see his visions for a large, new church in the offering.

Over the years, Miss Whitmire and Mr. Kroelinger became friends and she made several transfers to the church. Some of these transfers would have initially gone to a university; however, she redirected the gift to the church. Because Miss Whitmire began spending her winters in Clearwater, where the church was to be located, Mr. Kroelinger had an opportunity to see her everyday and talk over his plans for a shiny new building. It is alleged that he entered into a deliberate campaign to make her generosity finance his ambitious plans. He did this, apparently, by suggesting that her plans would be necessary in order to keep up with the Presbyterians, the Methodists and the Episcopalians in Clearwater. It was further alleged that upon realizing her natural bent and the influence that he had gained over her, he had the opportunity to enforce his will upon her.

The court stated that it must not be misled by proof of eccentricity; that to put it succinctly, a person has a legal right to be eccentric. Human actions, whether by manner of life or by deeds of legal import, may be eccentric and unusual, that fact does not mean that they, as a matter of law, are the results of undue influence. It further stated that it is not influence merely, but *undue* influence, that is always alleged — something excessive and unlawful, something which destroys free agency.

Undue influence generally has its origin in certain well-recognized classes of human relations out of which influence grows by reason of the relationship itself, such as father and child, mother and child, attorney and client, trustee and cestui que trustent, doctor and patient and religious advisor and people subject to religious appeals.

The court said that undue influence, in its last analysis, depends upon the facts of each individual case. But in proof of this undue influence, one must so clearly establish the existence of confidential relations as to throw the burden of proof as to a particular transaction upon the beneficiary (recipient of gift). In other words, when the complaining party shows that the beneficiary stood for a considerable period of time in a trusted relationship and had the opportunity to exercise influence, then the burden of explaining the good faith of the transactions thereafter occurring to that person's benefit or that organization's benefit fall upon the beneficiary. An influence which is considered undue is one which is exerted upon the grantor of a gift in order to override his/her will and make the act of executing the deed a mere mechanical performance.

However, a capricious or unreasonable disposition will not be set aside on that ground. There is no lawful objection to a will because it does not dispense with the testator's property to his heirs or relations, especially remote ones, unless deceitful arts have been used to estrange fixed affections.

The court states that where a prior fiduciary relation exists, the court will presume confidence placed and influence exerted; where no fiduciary relation existed, the confidence and influence must be proved by extrinsic evidence. Influence must have been acquired and abused or reposed and betrayed.

Wherever two people stand in such relation to one another, confidence is necessarily reposed by one and influence naturally grows out of that confidence. And where this confidence is abused or exerted to obtain an advantage, the person availing him/herself of his/her position will not be permitted to retain the advantage, although the transaction could not have been impeached if no such confidential relation had existed. In conclusion, the court states that the principle is applicable whenever there is a relation of trust and confidence, no matter from what cause it arises.

(2) **Cotcher's Estate**, 274 Mich. 154 (1936).
Hanna Cotcher died in 1932, a childless widow. The only relatives surviving her were one brother and three children of a deceased nephew. She wrote her will in 1930, leaving one-third to the Holy Family Orphanage Home of Marquette and the remaining two-thirds to the pastor of St. Peter's Cathedral in Marquette to be used

for a particular school. The court recounts certain facts about her life — including that she was a Catholic but married to a Protestant, and that during her married life she went to church rarely, if at all.

After the death of her husband, however, she resumed her religious beliefs and became a practicing Catholic. Her husband had accumulated considerable real estate which she inherited. During the time period from 1925 to 1930, she made three wills, each of which makes the same provisions for the children of her nephew. The final will was prepared by the attorney for the Bishop of the Roman Catholic Church.

The question presented here was whether Hanna Cotcher was a free agent in planning and executing her final will or whether it was the result of the influence of another. The court found that there was a confidential and fiduciary relationship between the pastor and Mrs. Cotcher, which gave rise to the presumption of undue influence. The pastor got to know her in 1925 and in the summer of 1929 he saw her in her own flat, and talked to her about getting into a home. In general, he preached to the members of his church to provide for themselves after death. The court states, "There appears to be no dispute over the fact that Father Buchholz did nothing directly to influence testatrix." However, the court sets a standard that in order to establish undue influence there is a presumption of such where a person devises property to one standing in a confidential and fiduciary relationship to the testator. This presumption is rebuttable.

The court also states that it has held in the past that some influence may be properly used, and that it is only when the testator's will is overcome is the result of the disposition invalid. Mrs. Cotcher was urged and solicited to support the church and its charities while she attended church, but the solicitations were not individual, they were made to all parishioners alike. This method of raising money for churches and charities, the court stated, prevails throughout all Christendom. There can be no inference of undue influence from its use alone. Therefore, the court found that the urgings of Father Buchholz did not go beyond the teachings of the church and that the will of testatrix was not overcome by this doctrine. It also found the fact that her lawyer and other subscribing witnesses were Roman Catholics did not raise any inference or presumption of undue influence.

(3) **Estate of Reilly vs. Sisters of Charity,** 479 Wash. 1 (1970). Miss Reilly was born in 1887 and was educated in private schools. She was described as being thorough and accurate in keeping accounts of her investments, although she was quite secretive concerning her financial and personal affairs. Others testified that she had a strong mind and was not easily influenced. Miss Reilly did not marry.

In 1963 she consulted a doctor regarding swelling of the glands in her neck, and it was diagnosed as Hodgkin's Disease. The report showed malignant lymphoma. After a serious episode, the doctor sent her to Providence Hospital. Miss Reilly moved to the home where the doctor saw her from time to time.

Miss Reilly's half-brother had, in the past, after their father's death, instituted an action against Miss Reilly. He claimed that she embezzled certain stocks belonging to the father's estate with the intent to defraud her half-brother. In the claim against her will, the claimants said that her will was unnatural because she did not make bequests to various Catholic charities, and only gave to the home. The trial court had found a fiduciary relationship existed between Miss Reilly and the Sisters of Charity because she had gone to the home to die and that she was a helpless old woman without any close relatives.

The appellate court was not entirely convinced that this was true. However, it did state that there was nobody else with primary concern for her welfare. The court set as its standard that the contestants had the burden of proof to show by convincing evidence that testatrix had made her will under undue influence by another person.

The court reports considerable testimony between one particular sister and Miss Reilly regarding gifts to the home and her need to draw a will. However, this alone would not be sufficient to show undue influence. It is important that (1) the beneficiary of the gift occupy a fiduciary or confidential relation to the testator, (2) that the beneficiary actively participate in the preparation or procurement of the will and (3) that the beneficiary receive an unusually or unnaturally large part of the estate.

Whether a will is natural or unnatural is a question to be determined by the facts of each case. A will is considered unnatural when it is contrary to what the testator, from his/her known views, feelings and intentions would have been expected to make. In Miss Reilly's situation, she had not heard from her half-nephew and nieces for twenty-eight years. The court said, "They had no claim on her bounty."

The contestants made much of the fact that the sister stated to employees of the home that a wealthy lady was coming there and they should treat her well because she might leave something to the home. It was also alleged that the sister told Miss Reilly that she must make her will, and that this was repeated several times. At one point, the sister said to another person at the home, "We finally got Miss Reilly to make out a will." The court notes that "even where solicitation is made for a specified bequest, this does not constitute undue influence unless it be so importunate, persistent, coercive or otherwise so operates to subdue the will of the testator and deprive him/her of freedom of action. Influence exerted merely by means of advice, argument, persuasion, solicitation, suggestion or entreaty is not undue influence."

The court also did not find undue influence in the fact that the attorney for Miss Reilly was the attorney for the home. The contestants claimed that she lacked testamentary capacity and, in addition, there was a confidential relationship between the attorney and her. The court noted that she told the attorney of her existing will leaving everything to contestants, which had been drawn up by a former attorney. The home's attorney offered to telephone the former attorney, but Miss Reilly vetoed that suggestion. Later, Miss Reilly gave the telephone number, and included further information regarding where the key to her safe deposit box was. The court said that such actions did not support a finding of lack of testamentary capacity.

It said that the term *undue influence* cannot be given a definition that will serve as a safe and reliable test in every case, that each case depends to a large degree upon its own facts. It further said that not every influence exerted over a person can be undue influence. Proof of solicitation, persuasion, suggestion, advice or entreaty is not enough to warrant revoking the probate of a will on the ground of undue influence. Such influence must be proven by evidence that is clear, cogent and convincing. In reviewing cases where undue influence was found, it said that in each case (1) the testator had little or no mental capacity, (2) the testator was greatly impaired physically, (3) the testator disinherited one near and dear to him/her or (4) the estate or a major portion thereof was devised or bequeathed to one with whom the testator had no close ties.

A dissenting judge made a different case. He noted that the trial court found Miss Reilly's will null and void. He stated that the home had a confidential relationship with testator, and therefore, the burden was on the beneficiary to show that the will was not procured by undue influence. He said that this "rich woman" was indeed treated very well by the home. She was given a special room redecorated to conform to her every desire. In addition, the attorney to the home had been the longtime legal advisor to the nursing home and was procured by the home to draw the will. He further points out that although Miss Reilly had not seen her half-brother for many years, there was no enmity after he had brought suit against her. He also points out that the nieces and nephews were beneficiaries under prior wills. He did admit, however, that the nieces and nephews had not had contact with Miss Reilly for many, many years. However, he blamed that on her moving around. His major point was that he felt it appeared clear from the record that the home did not become a significant object of any giving on the part of Miss Reilly until after she had taken up residence there, was ill with terminal cancer and was exposed to the repetitive solicitations of the sisters.

What standards can we draw from these cases? If these factors are present, undue influence may be occurring:

A.   Confidential relationship
B.   Participation in procuring the will
C.   Unusually or unnaturally large part of the estate
D.   Age/condition of health
E.   Opportunity to exert influence
F.   Unnaturalness of the objects of bounty

See the following newspaper articles for examples of more current cases.

$6.6 Million 'Saga of Deceit'
Church Told to Repay Heiress

United Press International
Worcester, Mass.

A fundamentalist church must return $6.6 million to an heiress who was manipulated into donating the money through an "astonishing saga of clerical deceit," a federal bankruptcy judge ruled yesterday.

U.S. Bankruptcy Judge James Queenan Jr. ruled that Elizabeth Dayton Dovydenas, heiress to the Minneapolis-based retail chain Dayton Hudson Corp., can get back all the money she donated to The Bible Speaks church.

A three-week trial in U.S. Bankruptcy Court pitted Dovydenas, 34, against the church and its fundamentalist pastor, the Rev. Carl Stevens Jr., 57. The church is based in the Berkshire Mountains town of Lenox, Mass.

"This is a case of undue influence exerted upon a church donor, which appears to be unsurpassed in our jurisprudence in its variations and in the sums involved," Queenan wrote in his ruling.

"Revealed is an astonishing saga of clerical deceit, avarice and subjugation on the part of the church's founder, Carl H. Stevens," the judge wrote. "He has abused the trust of the claimant as well as the trust of many good and devout members of the church."

The trial, which featured tearful witnesses and eyebrow-raising glimpses into the lives of the privileged, concluded on April 16. The judge then took the case under advisement.

The attorney for The Bible Speaks, flamboyant New York lawyer Norman Roy Grutman, indicated that the church would have to close its doors if the ruling was in Dovydenas' favor.

Dovydenas and her husband, Jonas, a free-lance photographer, joined the church in 1981.

She testified that she came increasingly under the spell of Stevens, a strict religious fundamentalist.

"He was like a god to me," she testified. She said Stevens cut her off from family and friends who might counteract his influence.

Court papers indicated that part of the $6.6 million she donated was used to buy a $320,000 condominium in Palm Beach that contained floor-to-ceiling mirrors and a vibrating bed.

— From the *San Francisco Chronicle*, 1987

In a Second Case:

Court Upholds Ruling Against Deathbed Will, Limits Award

A physician connected with a religious sect improperly influenced a Sunnyvale woman on her deathbed to leave her property in his control, but a $2 million punitive damage award in the case was excessive, a state appeals court ruled yesterday.

A state Court of Appeal upheld a Santa Clara County jury's verdict setting aside the will and separate gifts of a van, a mobile home and a $121,500 trust deed to Anami Ashram.

The evidence showed that Dr. John Lovelace of San Jose, founder and vice president of the ashram, "pressured an elderly and extremely vulnerable woman into leaving the bulk of her estate under the control of Lovelace instead of her natural heirs," said Presiding Justice J. Anthony Kline.

But Kline said there was no evidence that the sect was part of a network of religious groups or had anywhere near the amount of property needed to pay a $2 million judgment. A new trial is needed to determine the amount of punitive damages that would properly punish the sect and deter others, the court said.

The case involved Marie Beth Covert, who died of cancer in April 1982 in a San Jose hospice at the age of 72.

— From the *San Francisco Chronicle*, 1987

The planned giving officer must also be aware of the potential for involvement in tax scams and schemes on two levels — one where s/he unknowingly accepts a gift involving some impropriety and the other where s/he willingly participates in a scam. The federal tax law provides substantial penalties for the latter.

The desire to help a donor or encourage a gift must be distinguished from getting involved in schemes which may be detrimental to both parties involved. There are more issues than known answers here.

What should a planned giving officer do if s/he knows a gift structure or plan is incorrect, but the donor is being advised by a CPA or an attorney?

What should s/he do as to gift acceptance if the donor insists on keeping the structure in an improper form and tells the planned giving officer it is not his/her business, it is between the donor and his/her advisor?

Should an organization pay a "finder's fee" for a charitable gift? This is a very touchy issue, but it seems to me that people should get paid for their service. It may, however, depend on the depth of the work. Some people frown upon the idea of a "finder's fee," so discuss the potential situations with your board and committees. What is and is not reasonable for services performed?

Take Fiduciary Responsibility Seriously

Another area to be concerned about is your fulfillment of fiduciary responsibilities. When an organization takes on the management of a donor's gift in trust, in annuity form or in insurance contract form, it takes on certain responsibilities. These responsibilities include twelve basic duties:

(1)   The trustee has a duty to administer the trust according to the trust instrument.

(2)   The trustee has a duty to administer the trust solely in the interest of the beneficiaries (the beneficiaries include both the life interest beneficiaries and the remainder beneficiary). Sales, exchanges or investments must be fair and reasonable with respect to both beneficiaries.

(3)   Where two or more beneficiaries are present, the trustee has a duty to deal with them impartially.

(4)   The trustee may not use or deal with the trust property

for the trustee's own benefit.

(5) The trustee has a duty to keep control of and to preserve the trust property.

(6) The trustee has a duty to make the trust property productive under the circumstances and in furtherance of the purposes of the trust.

(7) The trustee has a duty within a reasonable time to dispose of any part of the trust property, including property at the time of its creation, that would not be a proper investment for the trustee to make.

(8) The trustee has a duty to keep the trust property separate from other property not subject to trust and to see that trust property is designated as property of the trust.

(9) The trustee has a duty to take reasonable steps to enforce claims.

(10) The trustee has a duty to take reasonable steps to defend actions which may result in a loss to the trust.

(11) The trustee may not delegate the entire administration to another person (certain trustee duties may be delegated to an agent).

(12) Where there is more than one trustee, each trustee has the duty to participate in the administration of the trust.

The trustee must administer the trust with the care, skill, prudence and diligence under the circumstances then prevailing that a prudent person acting in a like capacity and familiar with such matters would use in the conduct of an enterprise of like character and with like aims to accomplish the purposes of the trust as determined from the trust instrument.

As to investing and acquiring or exchanging property, the trustee shall act with the care, skill, prudence and diligence under the circumstances then prevailing, including but not limited to the general economic conditions and the anticipated needs of the trust and its beneficiaries, that a prudent person acting in a like capacity and familiar with such matters would use in the conduct of an enterprise of like character with like aims to accomplish the purpose of the trust as determined from the trust instrument.

The trustee also has a duty to inform the beneficiaries of the trust activities and administration. State law generally provides that the trustee shall make an accounting, at least annually, to each of the beneficiaries to whom income or principal is required to be given at some point. The contents of such an accounting are often controlled in some detail by state law.

In addition to the typical fiduciary duties listed above, certain discretionary powers may be granted in a trust document.

A trust instrument giving discretionary powers may do so by conferring "absolute," "sole," or "uncontrolled" discretion to a trustee to act in accordance with certain fiduciary principles or stated objectives of the trustor. For example, in a charitable trust, a trustee may be given a "sprinkle power," designed to permit the trustee to exercise his/her discretion as to which of a class of beneficiaries should receive the yearly income from a charitable trust.

A charitable organization taking on the management of a donor's gift in trust, in annuity form or insurance form, has these duties in general, but more specifically must guard the charitable purpose and not jeopardize the corpus of the gift. Contributions made are considered to be held in "public trust." A general standard is applied requiring proper guarding of the assets in "public trust." The board of directors of an organization must seriously consider these fiduciary responsibilities when deciding to accept the role as trustee or manager of annuities for the benefit of individuals.

Concerning finder's fees, an organization should confront the issue of "buying" charitable remainders before someone comes along to sell one (refer to the NCPG Standards).

If you wonder why you should have written board policies regarding all of the above, think liability. An organization is made up of its individuals. Individuals have minds of their own and views of their own regarding all of the above topics. The organization is, however, an entity for legal purposes and must act as such. An organization only acts through its board of directors, officers and agents.

In order to achieve a standard view on the above topics, policies should be written outlining exactly what the board of directors believes to be the corporate or entity view with regard to each and every one of these topics. The failure to do so will result, in the long run, in some form of liability.

The entity is the body corporate of all the officers, directors and agents acting on behalf of the legal entity known as the corporation. Where the standards above are breached, it is the entity that suffers the greatest harm.

That harm may come in three different forms of liability.

(1) **Legal.** An entity has legal liability to the Attorney General of the state, its beneficiaries, its employees, agents, etc. Many persons may make a claim against an organization for breach of any of the above standards or duties. The IRS and the state taxing authorities are included in those to whom a liability may flow. Other state or federal agencies may be involved as well. Penalties, fines on particular persons and potentially, in the worst cases, loss of exemption, are the damages to bear.

(2) **Media liability.** Although the legal liability is an important concern, the organization may be able to pay a penalty of a dollar amount and continue its operations. However, in any case where a breach of any of the above has occurred, it is *always* a matter of public record. Therefore, media coverage will be a fact and it may be harsh.

To be tried in the media is not the same as being tried in a court of law or even by an administrative agency. The media can be highly unfair when it finds something of interest to sell its papers or to make its evening news a little bit more interesting. You should guard your position so as not to find yourself on the evening news.

(3) **Donor relations.** Whether the entity has incurred legal liability or media liability will have a greatly multiplied effect on donor relations. Either of the two types of liability can lead to years of repair of donor relations, trust, credibility and confidence.

In the event that a breach is alleged, a written board policy — which has over the years been adhered to firmly — will be of considerable help either with legal liability or media liability.

9

Selecting Products

There is no end in nature, but every end is a beginning.
— Ralph Waldo Emerson, *Words of Wisdom to Live By*

Your products continually work for you, ever renewing your efforts out in the field and supporting you back in the office. Make sure they fit your needs.

Before aggressively taking your planned giving program to your specified markets, be sure to prepare and carefully review the material to be distributed. Determine the target and mission of each piece, from brochures to newsletters. And remember, the first piece received by your prospect **is** what the prospect will know about the organization. First impression, lasting impression. So make your decisions carefully when choosing materials that represent you.

First, will your brochures be "canned" or "shelved," meaning customized or produced for more mass appeal? Several publishers provide pre-printed brochures with space only for the organization's name. Sometimes there is just a little space allowed for custom text.

Publishers also provide partially prepared brochures where the organization has space to insert text pertinent to its program. You need to decide how much space you need for customization or if you want to completely customize your brochures. Will companies help you with the text and can you handle the costs of customization?

Perhaps you will choose to produce this material by yourself. Be very careful. This author has seen organizations use whole sections, if not whole brochures, prepared by another organization. That may be viewed as plagiarism. Sometimes the staff person at the organization from which the material is borrowed says, "It is alright." But does the entity feel that way? What about when that staff person leaves?

Then again, how many ways can you explain unitrusts? Take a look at other brochures to avoid the very specific language used by another organization. Check to see if another organization's material is copyrighted. As much as you can, try to create your own turn of phrase, imagery and examples in describing your program or certain vehicles. There is a tongue-in-cheek saying, taking from one source is plagiarism, taking from two or more is research. Be careful.

Speaking of content, should brochures describe vehicles or should they be marketing tools?

One answer is that every organization should have a main, persuasive planned giving marketing piece describing activities and how to fund them (not which gift vehicles to use, but how much it costs to endow or provide current support). As a secondary portion of the same brochure, a very brief description of methods of giving should follow each activity or funding opportunity. (For more information the reader should request specialty, vehicle brochures or even word-processed text.)

Another answer is that brochures of all types should be marketing-oriented in their text, style and tone. They should be designed to follow the market segments developed in the initial and continuing marketing studies of the organization. They will be topical, according to sub-markets. You should be aware of the publishers that provide such materials.

You may also be interested in brochures designed as a "program." Several publishers design bequest or life insurance program brochures. In other words, you buy into a prepared method of "marketing" bequests. Sometimes the publisher has consultants who explain the use of their product to forge better results.

There are some other factors to consider when selecting and preparing brochures, other than determining when it is appropriate to identify a target market or go with a shotgun approach. As we have said, many decisions will revolve around cost. The size of the material should be decided in relation to technical versus marketing information. Take into consideration the tone, text, vocabulary or jargon — think about how educated your audience is.

What is the most effective format for your material? Question and answer, narrative or something else? Consider how the texture and quality of the paper your material is printed on will correspond to the expectations of your market. Glossy finishes are obviously more attractive, but also more costly. The same is true with the use of color on your brochure. Consider the geographic area, culture and / or style of your target market. If possible, use visuals and graphic design that this audience might find more appealing. Do not clutter your brochure with text. Certainly avoid using a small type size when marketing to an older age group.

In either purchasing or customizing publishing company brochures, be sure to allow ample lead time before printing. There should be plenty of time between text delivery to the publisher and the date the brochure needs to be available to the organization for mailing. Do all of this research in advance so your organization develops a routine of consistently meeting targeted deadlines. This also includes determining the method of shipment and response time. In customer service or support, always be prompt, polite and client sensitive. Define the responsibilities of staff members in this process, especially editorial content. Be prepared to adapt to changes in the writing of these brochures.

Like everything else, the purpose of mailing brochures must be understood before the expense is incurred. Brochures are communication, education, motivation and visibility pieces. Remember? Step Five of the marketing plan. All four of the prior steps have to be done **before** this. Cultivation and solicitation are not directly intended. That is Step Six. Cultivation and solicitation in planned giving should be personal. Be sure to express this philosophy to all parties and come to an agreement.

Newsletters used in the planned giving process are often

printed in bulk and distributed to donors and advisors. They too can be canned, customized or self-written. Again, determine the content, which is the primary message you hope to convey. Develop editorial themes, and whether the content is program or technically specific. Mixing both program and technical content is important in newsletters, but try to strike a focused balance.

Make sure your content is timely. Think marketing and think ahead. Assuming your newsletter is quarterly, choose and prepare topics with the future in mind. (See chapter 4 on marketing). Use photos to break up your text and leave space for current events and reports from your board or committees.

Like your seminars, the format of your newsletters should also be developed with the "Sandwich" form in mind. Introduce the program, wade into the technical aspects of planned gifts and then conclude with more, and exciting, news about your program.

The function of a newsletter, brochures and letters is to provide continual contact: to create a feeling of closeness or linkage, to create visibility and to provide education and motivation. It should make the reader feel comfortable when talking to the volunteer or staff person about some of the items covered in the newsletter. It should act as a door opener.

We said brochures should be developed for marketing in general, for target markets specifically and for follow-up explanation and education. Newsletters, on the other hand, are the shotgun piece. A little of everything for everyone, mailed to "everyone" (or however many pieces you can afford).

In preparing a newsletter for advisors, look for technical advice blended with tips on planning for clients and marketing their services to clients. Unless you have extremely good technical skills, I advise letting a professional or a company write your newsletter to advisors.

Software support for your office is critical.

The list of software that is intended to support your financial analysis of proposed and actual planned gifts is growing very long. While this is not advertising space, it is important for you to know at least some of the major applications in the marketplace. Aaron and Associates of Fenton, Missouri; Crescendo of Camarillo, California; The Planned Gift Companion of St. Paul, Minnesota; PG Calc of Cambridge, Massachusetts; Philanthrotec of Matthews, North Carolina; and Benefactor by View Plan of San Diego, California, are the bulk of the calculation types of software that are available. All work well, but they are very different. You should ask for a demo disk and try them out yourself.

PG Calc also offers support for the office in its management of pooled income funds software and its gift annuity management program. Each of these applications makes it possible to take these functions in-house and do them accurately.

Docs in a Box from LMNOP offers document assembly for all of the charitable gift vehicles, trusts, pooled income funds, gift annuities, etc., for attorneys, or to be prepared by the charity as a courtesy for the attorney, and for donor's attorney's approval. The application contains an extensive set of easy, narrative explanations about the gift vehicles, cover letters, an on-screen library of IRS rulings, documents, legislation and the like. It is available through Precept Press, the publisher of this book.

Educational seminars are too numerous to mention specifically here, but they are always listed by the National Committee for Planned Giving (NCPG) and the list is available by calling NCPG in Indianapolis, Indiana.

NCPG also has other materials available for the planned giving officer on request.

Also see the list of books in the Library References section of this book. This is only a start. The end of the book, but truly the beginning.

Library References

'Come to the edge,' he said. They said, 'We are afraid.' 'Come to the edge,' he said. They came. He pulled them... and they flew.
— Guillaume Appolinaire, *Words of Wisdom to Live By*

General Books

Arthur Andersen & Company, *Tax Economics of Charitable Giving*, Eighth Edition.

Ashton, Debra, *The Complete Guide to Planned Giving* (JLA Publications, Cambridge, MA).

Donaldson and Osteen, *The Harvard Manual* (Office of Planned Giving, Harvard University).

Galloway, *The Unrelated Business Income Tax* (Ronald Press, Wiley & Sons), Fourth Edition.

Hamlin, Petkun and Bednarz, 442 T.M., *Charitable Income Trusts* (Bureau of National Affairs, Portfolio, Washington, D.C.).

Hopkins, *The Law of Tax-Exempt Organizations* (Ronald Press, John Wiley & Sons).

Jordan, Ronald R., and Katelyn L. Quynn, *Planned Giving: Management, Marketing and Law*, 1994 (John Wiley and Sons, New York, NY).

Moerschbaecher, Lynda, *The Well-Planned Gift: Advanced Case Studies* (Lynda S. Moerschbaecher, San Francisco, CA).

Petkun, Hamlin and Downing, 435 T.M., *Charitable Remainder Trusts and Pooled Income Funds* (Bureau of National Affairs, Portfolio, Washington, D.C.).

Powell, Walter W., Ed., *The Nonprofit Sector, A Research Handbook* (Yale University Press, New Haven, CT).

Pusey, J. Michael, *Charitable Remainder Trusts for the Citizen and Foreign Investor* (J. Michael Pusey, Los Angeles, CA).

Sharpe, Robert F., *Before You Give Another Dime* (Sharpe & Co., Memphis, TN).

Sharpe, Robert F., *The Planned Giving Idea Book* (Sharpe & Co., Memphis, TN).

Stanford University, *R-Plan Manual.*

Stern, Sullivan and Schumacher, *Charitable Giving and Solicitation* (Prentice-Hall, one volume looseleaf).

Teitell, *Deferred Giving* (Taxwise Giving, Old Greenwich, CT, two-volume).

Teitell, *Charitable Lead Trusts* (Taxwise Giving, Old Greenwich, CT, one volume).

Teuller, Alden, *Practical Guide to Planned Giving 1994* (The Taft Group, Washington, D.C.).

Treusch and Sugarman, *Tax-Exempt Charitable Organizations* (ALI-ABA).

White, Douglas, *The Art of Planned Giving,* 1995 (Wiley Books, New York, NY).

Marketing Books

Bottom-up Marketing, by Ries & Trout, published by McGraw-Hill Book Co.

Changing Demographics: Fundraising in the 1990's, by Judith Nichols, published by Bonus Books, Chicago.

Contemporary Cases in Marketing, by W. Wayne Talarzyk, published by The Dryden Press, in many cities, one of which is San Francisco.

Managing Nonprofits, by Peter Drucker.

Marketing for Nonprofit Organizations, by Philip Kotler, published by Prentice-Hall, Englewood Cliffs, NJ.

Marketing Magic for Major and Planned Gifts, by Lynda S. Moerschbaecher, published by Precept Press, a Division of Bonus Books, Inc., Chicago.

Marketing Imagination, by Theodore Levitt, published by the Free Press.

Marketing Theory: Classic and Contemporary Readings, by Jagdish N. Sheth and Dennis E. Garret, published by South Western Publishing Company, Livermore, CA.

Marketing Warfare, by Ries and Trout, published by New American Library, New York City.

Marketing Your Products and Services Successfully, by Harriet Stevenson and Dorothy Otterson, published by Oasis Press, Milpitas, CA.

Positioning, by Ries and Trout, published by Warner Books, New York City. MUST READING, ENJOYABLE, TOO.

Strategic Marketing for Nonprofit Organizations, by Philip Kotler and Allan R. Andreason, published by Prentice-Hall, Englewood Cliffs, NJ.

Targeted Fund Raising, by Judith E. Nichols, published by Bonus Books (Precept Press), Chicago.

The Marketing Plan, by David S. Hopkins, published by the Conference Board, New York, NY.

The Popcorn Report, by Faith Popcorn, published by Harper Business (Harper Collins Publishers), New York.

Periodicals

Brownell, Catherine Ed., *Chronicle of Non Profit Enterprise* (Seattle, WA).

Chronicle of Philanthropy (Washington, D.C) Biweekly.

Hopkins, *The NonProfit Counsel* (Charitable Production Co., Inc., Washington, D.C.) Monthly.

Moerschbaecher, McCoy and Simmons, *Charitable Gift Planning News* (Little Brown & Co., Boston, MA) Monthly.

Meuhrcke, Jill, Ed., *Non Profit World* (Madison, WI). Stern, Larry Ed. *Non-Profit Times,* Princeton, NJ.

Schoenhals, Roger, *Planned Giving Today* (Roger Schoenhals, Seattle, WA).

The Taft Group, *The Planned Gifts Counselor,* (Washington, D.C.) Monthly.

Teitell, *Taxwise Giving*, (Taxwise Giving, Old Greenwich, CT) Monthly.

Lloyd, Charles E., *Trusts and Estates Magazine* (Atlanta, GA). Marketing.

Index

217